STRAIGHT TALK
FOR MEDICAL STUDENTS

STRAIGHT TALK
FOR MEDICAL STUDENTS

An Insider's Guide to Successfully Applying, Interviewing, and Surviving the First Year of Medical School

DR. RICHARD P. WINSLOW

For Jennifer

Table of Contents

Introduction

Nearly a decade ago, I stepped onto my first medical school campus as a higher education administrator. It would be a new experience for me, but not all that different from my other work in higher education. The blocking and tackling at a graduate school aren't very different than the X's and O's at an undergraduate college/university.

I did find some marked differences in the type of student who was seeking a master's degree and/or a medical degree, as their level of seriousness and commitment to their studies was markedly higher than most students at the undergraduate level. But the most significant difference between undergraduate and graduate education, that I quickly noticed, was in both the goals that students had for themselves and the end product that we produced as a university.

Being able to say that our product, our graduates, literally go on to save and change lives for the better reinforces a certain level of pride you have in doing your work each and every day you walked onto campus. It made me personally want to be at the top of my professional game because I was helping to educate and mold future physicians who would go on to impact lives all over this world with their professional talent and dedication. If I was able to model that professionalism for them, then they could learn from someone who genuinely cared and had high expectations for each of his students.

That was the beginning of my career in medical education. And since that first day on-campus I have learned so much about the dedication, sacrifices, commitment, and fire that it takes to navigate this experience successfully.

As you, the reader, prepares to make that big step, it is my hope that I can help prepare you as best as possible to be ready for the ups and downs of what is both an amazingly fulfilling and draining journey.

First, you should be commended for your desire to go down this path. It is a rare breed of human who dares to walk the halls of a university as a medical student. You represent less than 5% of the people in the world who want to become doctors and apply for entry. Assuming you make it through medical school and graduate, you will represent less than 1% of the people in the world who can be called doctor.

When you step in that rarified air of being a physician, you are also taking on the huge responsibility of literally having the lives of fellow human beings in your hands. That is an incredible burden that has both huge responsibility and incredible rewards. So, don't ever take this commitment lightly.

As a physician, you will walk along the human journey from the first breath of life, to the final breath that a human takes: the Alpha and the Omega of human existence. You will have the great honor of assisting in bringing life into this world. You will hold someone's newborn child in your hands for its first breaths in this world. And similarly, you will have the great privilege of holding a patient's hand as they experience their last moment on this earth, as they pass away.

The gravity of being present at the beginning and the end of life is punctuated by all of the moments you will share as a physician, at the in-between points of life, with your patients. First bouts with the flu, upper respiratory infections, first surgeries, first significant health diagnoses, and first terminal diagnoses. You will be a part of your patients' lives during very significant moments that they may not share with anyone else, but you. That, again, is an honor and a privilege and certainly nothing that you are entitled to experience. It is a privilege you will earn and continue to earn each day you practice medicine.

So, the stakes are high for you. You wonder why this is such a big deal, such a challenge, such a privilege? That is why.

You will hear something similar to this on your first day of medical school, reminding you that you have one shot at getting this thing right. You have one shot at becoming a doctor. Don't screw it up.

But just as with other professions, no one expects a brand-new medical student to know how to navigate such a complex educational journey on their own. The great news is that there are so many trained professionals that are there to help walk with you through the journey. Therefore, I wanted to write this book to provide a valuable resource for students making the important step towards going to medical school. Because the more advice and help one can get before you begin the journey the better off you will be, the fewer questions you will have to ask, the more details you will have before you even arrive, so that you can focus your life on the top priorities: academically excelling, absorbing the material you need to learn, and preparing the skills you need possess in order to become a successful doctor.

It's my belief that if my medical students were sitting in a room with you they would say something to the effect of (and I am paraphrasing here), "Dr. Winslow will tell you the truth. He is direct, honest, and won't mince words or advice in order to hurt your feelings or save your feelings from hurt. He will shoot straight with you." And so that is my approach in this book. Over 25+ years, I have learned to speak to students in, hopefully, a non-threatening, very direct manner about how their first-year works. I have also developed a clear understanding of what role the student plays in a successful transition from undergrad to medical school. In addition, I have also learned that the best outcomes for you usually occur when you set aside niceties and communicate directly about what works and what does not.

As you begin reading this book, it is my hope that you will visualize yourself in my office as we have a direct conversation about how to approach the first year. But before you read any further, do understand the following about this book: There will be parts of it that may make you uncomfortable for a variety of reasons. There will be parts of this book that may lead you to shake your head or doubt that I know what I am talking about. I do not ever claim to have the Wisdom of Solomon, nor do I claim to have every answer to each issue. But what I have learned I am sharing with you and if it makes you a little bit uncomfortable, so much the better. Sometimes discomfort is our brain telling us that maybe we need to rethink or reconsider something we may find uncomfortable. Medical school can be an uncomfortable process: Full of challenges, mystery, frustrations, and rarely possessing a comfort zone within which student can step.

Step out of your comfort zone and go on a journey with me that might not feel altogether secure. I promise you that at a minimum this book will reinforce the incredibly important role you play as a medical student, will make you think in different ways about what might or might not work well in that role, and will, I hope, lead to a healthier, more successful year for you.

Enjoy, take notes (there is a notes section in the back of the book), and don't be afraid to be a little nervous about what you are about to encounter. Nervousness keeps you honest and humble and those are two very good traits to possess as you set off on this journey.

CHAPTER 1

What a Medical Student Should Expect from This Book

I have worked with tens-of-thousands of graduate students wanting to get into medical school and many thousands of students who were accepted. Each of them possessed what I call their "origin story", the moment when they decided they wanted to become a physician. For many, it was a story that began a long time ago, when they were a child, and had a life-changing experience with a doctor. For some it began when a teacher inspired them to excel in the sciences. For some, it began with a conversation with their parents, where their parents encouraged them to consider medicine as a career.

Regardless of the origin story, almost every student I encountered wanted to excel and to succeed. They genuinely wanted to do the hard work to progress through school and become a physician.

If you are a student with an origin story and want to work hard to realize your dream, I am here to help you. The great thing about any educational experience is that you, the student, are in the driver's seat. You get to decide how you want to shape your path through medical school. You get to shape your own definitions for how to remain well, remain focused, and how you wish to define your happiness.

As I have developed hundreds of relationships with medical students during my career, one theme remains clear: There is nothing more unsettling for any medical student to have such a dream, and yet to be struggling in med school.

My goal in providing this resource to med students is not to understand and explain every single complex layer of the experience. That would be almost impossible or would lead to a resource that would be such a length that you would never have a chance to read it due to your busy, pre-med life. I don't think either of us would wish to read that book. Similarly, my goal is certainly not to anticipate and predict every dynamic that can act upon a medical student during their first year.

Rather, I first seek to share my experiences and the common themes that frequently emerge for medical students during that critical first year. And secondly, I wish to provide advice on how the student can create a goal, a plan, build an accountable relationship with themselves, and find success during what can be a really difficult journey both academically and personally.

Building an honest relationship with oneself that leads to success requires the following:

- Understanding the true reason(s) of why you want to be a physician in the first place.
- Being honest with oneself about what medical school attributes are priorities during your search process.
- Understanding the strengths and weaknesses you bring to the table when you are preparing your application.
- Practicing being your best, most authentic self when you interview.
- Becoming accepting of the fact that you will need to make sacrifices in order to be successful.
- Understanding that there are common pitfalls that are out there in front of you that you can fall victim to, but open enough to listen and learn how to be proactive to avoid such mistakes.
- Knowing you are making a conscious choice to join a profession that requires you to live a life of the highest levels of ethical, moral, and humanistic expectations.
- Steadfastly adhering to the oath you will take as a new medical student, as well as the oath that you will take the day you become a physician; to do good and to do no harm, ever.

You might be thinking or saying something like, "Does all of this need to occur during my first year of my time in medical school?

The answer is no, not necessarily. But the foundation for success needs to be laid during that first year. In my experience, the more comfortable you are in your skin, the more confident you are of your abilities, and the more aware you are of your weaknesses, the better off you will be in this initial year. If you lack that comfort, that self-awareness, and that self-acuity, the rest of your experience can result in problems. Your experience can be filled with problems, issues of adjustment, tension, stress, and potential lack of academic success before, during, and after your med school years. If these foundational attributes of oneself do not form around your experience, ultimately, when you graduate...or don't graduate...you will lack the personal and professional skills and the healthy balanced relationship with yourself that will aid you to be a meaningfully contributing professional beyond medical school and into the residency years.

Additional advice and guidance I intend to provide connects the personal relationship that you are building with yourself, to the day-to-day reality of the experience. This includes what it is like to be a medical student, the skills you need to develop and hone, as well as the common mistakes students make. They are able to predict, with some accuracy, what issues one might have during your first year are more successful in helping themselves to handle those issues in healthy, effective ways. For instance:

- Are you going to medical school for the right reasons?
- How do you prepare to get ready to enter to school?

- What conversations do you need to have with friends, family, and yourself, prior to leaving?
- How can you develop the attributes of resilience and grit and hone those attributes to assist you throughout your academic journey?
- What are the key attributes of students who are successful in the first year of medical school?
- What are the key survival characteristics that contribute to your well-being and personal and professional development during your first year?
- What are the most common mistakes made by medical students in year one?

What I ask from each reader, is to think about your own journey to get to this point. What has been working well for you? What parts of your own educational and personal journey could use changes? What personal biases do you bring to reading this book? Can you put those aside while you read? What parts of this book make you feel uncomfortable? Could your own discomfort be signaling something to you about the way you are approaching med school that needs to be reinforced or changed? I hope you will remain open to thinking about these questions as you move through the upcoming pages.

CHAPTER 2

Why You Wish to Accept This Challenge and Other Crazy Thoughts

Why Become a Physician?

You really are committed to this aren't you? You have had that urge to be a doctor since you were five, or nine, or 12, or 17, when you realized, for whatever reason(s), that you wanted to become a physician. And you have your own reasons for why, which we will discuss at greater length as we proceed.

But first, are you really sure? This is a path that is worthy of great, smart, dedicated people, of which you may be one. It is a path that results in fewer moments with friends, fewer moments with family, fewer fun times like vacations, three-day weekends, fewer baseball games, soccer matches, and time with your kids. This is a path that requires dedication, hard work, and unpleasantly long hours. This is a journey that can suck you in and spit you out.

Regardless of your reasons for wanting to be a physician, I encourage any student seriously becoming a doctor to understand the reasons not to be a physician first. The following should not be used as reasons for wanting to be a physician:

- **Money**—Money is one of the false prophets of medicine that sounds really good when you are thinking about the reward side of the job. But it should not be a driving force for why you wish to become a physician. The physicians I know and work with on a regular basis will acknowledge that they are paid at the top of the American professional pay scale, but in actuality, as they become immersed within the American medical system, the money almost never eclipses the professional challenge and reward.

- **Prestige**—There is no doubt that the title "Doctor" carries with it some cache. In our society, doctors are highly respected (even though nurses have now eclipsed physicians on the most trusted profession list). But most physicians will admit that this is not a reason to enter a profession.

- **Parents**—I cannot count the number of times I have had a difficult conversation with a struggling medical student, who is choking back tears and saying, "I didn't want to be a doctor. It was my parents who wanted me in medical school." Your parents don't have to live with a life-long professional commitment. You do. Don't go because your parents want you to go. You either choose to do this for yourself or don't do it.

- **Debt**—More than likely, you will accrue a lot of financial debt in order to become a physician. According to the American Association of Medical Colleges (AAMC), students, on average, borrow approximately $200,000 in order to become a physician. Seventy-six percent of students borrow some amount of money from the federal government in order to pay for it. Do not assume this financial burden on unless you are absolutely sure that you want to do this, as you will have a large mortgage-like payment awaiting you in four years' time.

- **Burnout**—A recent American Medical Association (AMA) study indicates that over 50% of physicians will reach levels of burnout that are unhealthy both personally and professionally. Because of the massive amount of stress that physicians are under at work and at home, burnout now occurs frequently. If you are one that does not cope well with stress and burnout, medicine may not be your best professional pick.

- **State of our Medical System**—Let's be honest with one another, the state of both our national medical system and our medical insurance system is a disaster. We see it almost daily on the national news. The costs of medical procedures, the costs of medication, the anxiety of medical coverage: it all indicates that our medical system is on the verge of either significant change or significant and swift collapse. If you cannot see yourself working in such a system, don't make the decision to go.

What are the real, legitimate reasons for becoming a physician? It is important to note that just because there are legitimate reasons for not joining a profession, there are certainly many sincere reasons for wanting to go into medicine. Some of the following form the healthier reasons for desiring a career in medicine:

- **Helping Others**—I love reading applications because one of the most talked about reasons for wanting to become a physician is the human desire to help those in need. The stories run the gamut in terms of time and place, but the bottom-line message is the same: I want to help others. It is an amazing reason for desiring to enter a profession and one that carries with both sincere emotion and empathy. A piece of advice: Do not let your emotion and empathy be the sole drivers for such a decision. Think about the other non-emotive reasons for this choice.

- **Love and Fascination with Science**—I have a friend who is an accomplished physician (pulmonologist), who lost a parent early in his life. Reading science books was his way of coping with the loss of his father. His nightly

WHY YOU WISH TO ACCEPT THIS CHALLENGE

reading developed into a passion for science and led him to his career as an accomplished doctor and flight surgeon. For many students considering med school, the root of that interest lies in a passion found in science.

- **Fascination with the Human Body**—Similar to those who have a love for science, many students find themselves with a keen interest in the human body and how it works. Usually I hear stories about first dissections of frogs and pig hearts, which led to an unending interest in biology class and a desire to take an anatomy course in college. All of this interest in the human body forms a great motivation when students are learning about the systems of the body in year one.

- **Job Stability**—It is true that medicine is a recession-proof career. But so is nursing and many other medicine/health care related fields. There is no doubt that once you reach the height of a doctorate level degree, job loss is a very small possibility. Don't let this be the only reason why you decide to be a doctor. It should be an added benefit, but not the driving reason behind the choice!

- **Always Wanted to Do This**—This final category of reasons usually possesses a bit of all of the above in the thought process behind why one chooses this profession. For these students, they have the desire to help others, the passion for science, a desire to learn more about the human body, and the inner drive to succeed. And most of these types of students will say, when asked, "I have just always had a drive to do this. When I think about the reason why I want to be a physician, there are many reasons why…." They then spend a little while telling you all of their reasons for wanting to be a physician. They get the big picture and the small reasons why one would choose this profession. And they are able to articulate it in a meaningful way.

I do not claim to know every legitimate reason for wanting to be a physician. I share this abbreviated list for two reasons: 1) These are the most common reasons I hear from students when I discuss with them why they want to become a physician. Some make sense. Other, perhaps, don't. Starting with a general barometer to help you determine whether your reason(s) are legitimately sincere and credible might be helpful as you make this decision. 2) You need to think beyond your initial analysis for such a huge decision. You are literally making a decision that will have ripple effects far into your future. Make sure you are thinking of as many variables as possible before you make your final decision. If you have thought through as many variables as possible and still decide to become a physician, good for you. You have at least performed your due diligence.

Getting Your Ducks in a Row to Go to Medical School

Monumental decisions, such as taking the long, difficult road forward, require you to begin thinking about why you wanted to become a physician earlier in life than say a profession such as a financial advisor or becoming a higher education administrator (like me). That doesn't mean those career choices are bad, it just means that becoming a physician requires one to begin to prepare your path much earlier in life than those other career options.

Believe it or not, for those students who know you want to become a physician, you really should begin thinking about it and the steps you need to take beginning in late middle school and early high school. Medical schools host "Doctor for a Day" programs across the country, where they intentionally bring eighth and ninth graders to campus to experience what it means to be a student physician in training. Part of that curriculum is intentionally focused on this age group, because they need to begin planning and making decisions in high school that will benefit their chances for getting into a quality undergraduate institution and a Pre-Med program.

Students who are in 8th or 9th grade should keep the following in mind as you begin your high school journey:

AP vs. Regular Coursework—I talk with a lot of students and parents about whether there are great benefits to taking Advanced Placement (AP) coursework during high school. The general gut reaction from most parents is, "You should be in AP courses because it shows you are smarter and more advanced as a student." This assumes you do well and get straight A's in those AP courses. If you get B grades or lower in the AP course, you can potentially do yourself more harm than good.

Colleges and universities who are looking for high school pre-med students are looking for students who show consistent, exceptional work in their high school science coursework. That means course grades of A- and above. For the vast majority of students, I recommend that if they want to become a Pre-Med major in college to not take AP coursework. Get all A's in your regular science classes. That boosts your GPA and will show "A" coursework throughout the science curriculum on your transcript. That has more weight in a transcript admission decision than spotty, inconsistent grades in AP courses.

Science Focus—High school is the time/place where students should begin to demonstrate their focus on science courses and a passion for science. I would recommend any student seriously considering becoming a physician (or a career in medicine/health care) to approach your science faculty at your high school to sit down with you and discuss the choices you need to consider and priorities you should consider in terms of coursework. High schools, most of them at least, have a set of courses that are options for students. You obviously are required to complete so many science courses in order to graduate. But most also have a limited number of courses that are available for students who want to push themselves and learn more. Seriously consider these courses and talk with a member of the faculty about your options.

Becoming a Leader—Colleges and universities don't want to accept students who have just solely focused on science. This also is a preview to what you can expect when you apply. They want to see that you have a passion for, and the grades in science. But they also want to see that you have begun developing yourself as a leader. For example:

- **Athletic Teams**—Are you a team member on one of your high school athletic teams? If so, you need to highlight this activity. If you aren't but are considering joining a team, I would encourage you to do so. It demonstrates a willingness to compete, improve an athletic skill, and a desire to work as part of a team. These are all skills you will need in both undergrad and in graduate school.

- **Clubs and Organizations**—In addition to activity in sports, join additional clubs and organizations. It shows that your interests are not one dimensional and will give you experience working for a cause, learning about something you don't know anything about, and/or becoming a leader in a different way than you already have on-campus.

- **Leadership Roles**—Now that you have decided to play sport and join some additional clubs/organizations, there is now an opportunity for you to lead in other ways. I would encourage you to run for some office or offer to be selected within your organization's leadership.

These are great examples that you can share on your application for undergrad, plus they give you leadership experience that you can take with you for the rest of life, including med school. Student Council? French Club president? Science Club treasurer? These are all great examples of opportunities that you can pursue.

- **Community Service**—Community service should be a part of any student portfolio beginning in middle and high school and continuing through year four. One critical component to demonstrating a desire to help others and a desire to help a developing community is through service. I encourage students find a non-profit that they are passionate about helping. There are countless organizations looking for young adults who can assist through volunteering. Students can also focus some of their energy on those organizations that serve their communities through healthcare and medicine. These always enhance a college application.

- **Physician Shadowing**—Physician shadowing is an opportunity a student gets with a local physician to "shadow" or follow the physician for a day at their office. Shadowing is unfortunately being done less and less these days because of HIPAA (Privacy) laws and legal liability related to practicing medicine. If you are able to identify a local doctor who is willing to allow you the chance to "shadow" once or even regularly, take this opportunity, as these are now a rare commodity. Keep track of who you shadowed, the date, time, and the name and address of the practice. These are all details you will need to put in your application for undergrad and medical school.

Your time in college/university is really when your serious steps towards med school are taken. During high school, you began to think about the reasons why you wish to be a physician. You have considered those variables and you have made the decision to move to the next step on the path.

Each college/university has their own way of teaching their science curriculum and each institution has a pre-designed path for students interested in the sciences to take that interest and apply it towards a Pre-Med pathway. There are definitely key variables you must organize and understand before selecting where you wish to apply:

Remaining Active—First and foremost, you are going to want to stay engaged during your undergraduate years. Focus on your science courses, but also remain involved in student organizations and take active leadership in those organizations. Colleges and universities will have even more opportunities to get involved. Take these and run with them.

Collecting Key Data for Applications—You will want to collect all the information about how you got involved in the classroom and outside the classroom as well. Keep information on your leadership positions, significant leadership initiatives that you took part in, and any work and/or shadowing you did during your undergrad years. These are going to be important data points that you will need to pull together on your applications.

Reviewing Prerequisites—Make sure you do your homework on the pre-requisites that you must complete in order for your application to be able to be reviewed. Both of the national application services for allopathic and osteopathic schools will require details about what courses you took, the title of the course, course number, and course description to insure you meet each school's requirements.

These requirements are easily found on each medical school's website. Do note that they vary by school. Make sure you pay attention to each school you plan to apply to in order to ensure that you meet their requirements. Typically, the following course requirements are standard pre-requisites for entry to medical school:

- **One year of Biology**—These course(s) are the foundation for everything you will encounter in years one and two.

- **One year of Chemistry**—Most schools will prefer that you have a biochemistry course, so if you can, do complete that course. It lays an additional foundation for biochemistry that you will take in years one and two.

- **One year of Physics**—Physics helps us understanding the forces that are at play within the human body and will ultimately perform a role in some treatments that utilize radiation, etc. You will need to know this.

- **At least one semester of Mathematics**—Medical analytics is a fast-growing field within medicine and is a course that is now popping up in many schools across the nation. Schools are going to expect you to have a working knowledge of calculus and/or statistics because so much of medicine now is being dominated by statistical analysis. Oh, and you also have to do math when calculating dosages for medications. Math is important…you will actually use it later in life, contrary to popular opinion.

- **One year of English**—If I were to identify one area where medical students could improve exponentially, it would be in the area of English, creative writing, and use of proper grammar. I read student's personal statements, within their applications, for a living and I am shocked at how poorly written they are, given that all of them are from seniors in college who desire to be physicians. Quality writing is part of critical thinking. And critical thinking is something that more and more med schools are beginning to push and expect from their students. Don't skip English because you think you are going to spend a career in the sciences. And, by the way, good writers are good communicators. And doctors need to be good communicators.

- **Preference for Biochemistry**—I shared above that most schools would prefer to see biochemistry as a part of the list of courses completed successfully.

- **Preference for Psychology/Sociology**—Part of critical thinking and developing into a good communicator is taking courses that apply to the humanistic part of medicine. Psychology and sociology are two courses that will win you points with admission committees, because it shows them that you have a desire to focus on humanism as a part of your education.

- **Preference for Anatomy**—One of the clear delineating lines I see in medical school lies between the students who have had an anatomy course (comparative or human), during their undergraduate years, and those who didn't. Those who have taken anatomy tend to perform better than those who have had none. If your school does provide an option for a human based anatomy course, I would highly recommend you take the course. You won't regret having a leg up on your fellow students once you arrive.

Consistent Contact and Communication with an Advisor or Advising Committee—The person or persons that are going to play a huge role in helping you get in will be your academic advisor and/or your Pre-Med Advising Committee. Each undergraduate institution approaches advising Pre-Med students a little differently. Some students are assigned a single, science-based faculty member. Some students are assigned a Pre-Med advising committee, made up of three or four science-based faculty members who oversee all advising for applicants. Or, in some rare occasions, students are assigned an individual advisor, but are also expected to meet regularly with their Pre-Med committee on a regular basis.

Regardless of the model, I would encourage you to plan to meet with your advisor(s) regularly. In that first meeting, take in your plan for your study schedule and your plan for success. Have your advisor look it over and provide feedback to you. This will be a good positive start to that relationship and you will come out of it with good advice.

Typically, they will be expected to meet with you once a semester to go over the next semester's course schedule and sign off on your registration for courses. Go beyond that individual appointment with your advisor(s). Try and meet with one or more of them once or twice more per semester. Stop in and say hello. Take a list of questions you may have developed. I have always found that in most cases, advisors are helpful and likely have the important answers to your questions. I promise, the more time you take to build a relationship with your advisor(s), the more it will pay off positively when it comes to application time.

Shaping Your Decision—There is a bit of homework you need to be doing in the lead up to your application. It's important homework that will help you shape how you apply, where you apply, and what to include in your application.

Types of Curricula—One of the biggest variables you need to consider when selecting where you will go to med school is based upon the type of curriculum the school uses as the foundation for how they teach medicine to their students. There are hours of student-led discussion, online, about the best approaches to teaching medical students. At the heart of those discussions is the role that the curriculum plays.

There are several different types of medical curricula that exist at universities:

- **Systems Based**—Systems-based curricula are just how they sound. They are designed to address the various systems within the human body. Most schools who use a systems-based approach teach the normal functions of the various body systems in year one of the curriculum. Then in year two of the curriculum, they teach the pathology of each system. This gives students a review of each system twice before they begin to apply the clinical aspects of the systems during clinical clerkship rotations in years three and four of the curriculum.

- **Case Based (CBL)/Problem Based (PBL)**—CBL/PBL curricula work off the premise that utilizing clinical cases to highlight the teaching of the body systems is the best approach to teaching and learning. This approach highlights the learning of the body systems, but rather than just focusing on the systems from a science perspective, does so in a clinical case-based manner that highlights systemic problems that occur within the clinical realm.

- **Modified Systems**—The newest approach is to combine the best of a systems approach (learning each system from both normal and pathological perspectives), while adding in the clinical case-based perspectives so that students pick up on clinical realities. Modified Systems Approach is the melding of both of the major curricular approaches.

Assessment of Competence—In addition to the type of curriculum used by the institution, students should also be considering how they will be assessed on their mastery of both course material, and clinical performance. Most schools grade students' performance via exams that are graded in the traditional A, B, C, F grading rubric. Anything under 70% is considered a failing grade.

Some other schools have moved to a Pass/Fail grading rubric where students no longer receive a grade of "A-F", but rather receive a Pass/Fail grade. Anything 70% or above is considered a "Pass". Anything below 70% is considered a "Fail".

There is much debate over which approach is not only the healthiest for students and the stress and pressure they feel about high stakes exams, but also how residency programs interpret "Passing" grades versus a more detailed letter grade. The debate is on-going.

How Courses Are Taught—Separate from the curricular content is the ways in which the content is delivered from a scheduling perspective. Each school has its own approach. Some students prefer being in class the entire time. Some want the freedom to study content from home. Some students want the flexibility to do both. Then one big question all students want answered is whether the school has a class attendance policy that ties them to attending every lecture.

Many schools teach using a block schedule approach. For example, courses are taught in a block of time each morning, with clinical courses or labs being taught in the afternoon. Block scheduling is a less flexible approach from students' perspectives, as it ties them to campus for long periods of time without the flexibility to gain access to the course content other than through class.

Many schools have a non-blocked schedule where courses are offered throughout the day and in a more specific order so that students can pick and choose what they attend and what they do not attend.

Either way courses are offered, they are likely juxtaposed, from a scheduling perspective, with the clinical courses that students are required to take. Either the morning will be filled with clinical coursework, or the afternoon. It is simply a matter of scheduling from a faculty perspective.

Finally, but probably most importantly to students is whether the school requires class attendance. If you are a student who wants a high level of freedom and flexibility in the way you prepare for and attend class, you probably don't want to attend a school that requires you to be in class every day. This is something you will need to consider as you examine and compare at the different schools you are considering. (I have my own professional opinion regarding class attendance that I will share with you later.)

Allopathic Versus Osteopathic—One of the most common questions I receive from students applying is focused on the differences between allopathic and osteopathic medicine. Students often have questions about what the differences are between osteopathic and allopathic medicine.

Osteopathic medicine is based upon four key principles: 1) the body is a unit of mind, body, and spirit; 2) the body is able to regulate, heal, and maintain itself; 3) the structure and the function of the body are mutually interrelated. These guiding principles are at the heart of each college of osteopathic medicine's curriculum.

Allopathic medicine's foundation is based in scientific-based model of modern medicine that utilizes medicines and surgery to treat patient's symptoms and illnesses.

First, are there differences in how these two groups are trained? To be completely honest, there is not much to differentiate the two. DOs are trained in almost the exact same ways as MD physicians today. They take the same kinds of courses, receive similar simulated clinical training, participate in the same types of clinical rotations during years three and four (often with MD students who train side-by-side with them). There are very few differences in the type of training DOs receive.

Formerly DOs chose primary care residencies at a significantly higher rate than MDs. One of the top osteopathic schools used to brag that 75% of their graduates went into primary care after graduation. That number, at the same school, in the last 6 years, has dropped from 75% to 45% simply because its students are competing for non-primary care residencies at such a higher rate. This is a changing dynamic and will ultimately result in both types of medical schools producing the same percentages of physicians going into primary care specialties.

DOs do receive additional training in Osteopathic Manipulative Techniques (OMT), also referred to as OMM (Osteopathic Manipulative Medicine). Allopathic students do not receive training in OMM. This training is centered upon the idea that the physician can manipulate the musculoskeletal system to insure proper skeletal alignment and activation of the lymphatic system. OMM is not chiropractic medicine.

OMM is an area of scientific research which is still growing in terms of the number of studies that are currently underway. Just like with any area of treatment, students have a wide-ranging number of opinions about OMT. Based upon my own anecdotal experience, if you were to ask a group of 100 osteopathic medical students how seriously they take OMM, approximately 25% would say that take it very seriously and want to use it in their daily practice of medicine. Fifty percent would say they take the course because it is required to graduate. And an additional 25% would say they have no intention of using OMM as part of their daily practice of medicine. It really is up to you, as the medical student to decide what you believe about your own OMM experience should you end up at an osteopathic school.

The presence of OMM in the DO curriculum does have one great advantage: I am convinced that one of the reasons DO physicians are so good at connecting with their patients, from a humanism perspective, is because of the extra training in OMM where they work very closely with patients in a hands-on, no pun intended, appropriate way.

If one looks at the average college GPA and average MCAT scores of students who attend allopathic and osteopathic universities, you will discover that scores run slightly lower for both quality indicators at osteopathic schools. That said, when you look at the quality of graduates and how they performed on the physician licensing exams, the USMLE and the COMLEX, the DO candidates who take USMLE score mostly consistent with MD candidates. Therefore, the end product is equally as good and consistent regardless of the type of school attended.

The DO degree is the fastest growing segment of the medical education market. According to Young, Chaudhry, Pei, Arnhart,

Dugan, & Snyder (2018), DOs used to represent about 5% of all physicians nation-wide. That number has increased to approximately 9% in 2018 with projections showing that the number will increase to approximately 17% of the physician market in the next five years. That number will grow steadily for the foreseeable future, as osteopathic universities are growing at rates much greater than those of allopathic schools.

Single Accreditation and Residency Match—One significant change that is occurring on the MD and DO landscape is the move to a single accreditation and residency match process. The MD students used to have their own residency application and match process. The DO students had their own application and process as well. The year 2020 will be the first year where those two processes will be brought together into a single process which includes both MDs and DOs. There may be much consternation about this new approach depending upon who you ask.

The bottom line is that all medical students will compete for jobs via the same selection process. The long-term outcome of this new combined match process will be good for medicine, good for medical students, and good for future patients. The short-term results of the new process remain, however, to be seen, but my best guess is that it will have a short-term, negative impact for some DO students and universities. That said, though, I don't think the negative impact will be large enough to recommend that you not attend an Osteopathic school.

This change is being made, in part, to communicate to the nation that there is no difference between DO and MD candidates. And I truly believe that will be the outcome once the dust settles.

New Horizons: The Future in the Medical School Classroom—One of the themes you will hear throughout this book is the fact that medical education is moving at the speed of light in terms of the development of course material and how medical students are being taught. Virtual reality is one of the new hot trends in medical education now. The use of digital images to mimic the human body is groundbreaking and certainly interesting from a visual perspective. But the jury is still out on virtual reality replacing the use of the human body, that is, cadavers to best teach students.

There is on-going debate about how these new technologies will impact teaching at the med school level. Simultaneously, there is continuing concern that as soon as one technology is introduced to the classroom, it is obsolete and has been replaced by a newer, more advanced technology. Medical education experts will have to wrestle with these realities as they decide how courses like Anatomy and clinical skills will need to be taught now and in the not-so-distant future.

Applying to Both Types of Medical Schools—If you do your homework, you will eventually come to know which type of school you prefer. That said, my students will tell you that I always preach having Option A, Option B, and Option C, as acceptance is never guaranteed.

The bottom line, therefore, becomes, your application to both types of schools. You need to have your top pick and then a backup plan. This back-up plan applies to both osteopathic and allopathic schools (the type of school) and the myriad schools within each grouping of schools. If your primary goal is to get into an osteopathic medical school, then your back up should be a grouping of allopathic schools, and vice versa.

MCAT Preparation—First and foremost, it's important that I share with you that I am not an expert on taking the MCAT. There are plenty of experts out there that provide courses on how to improve you MCAT score(s). I am not going to waste your time providing you with a list of things to do that will help increase your score. What I will do is provide you with some advice on things to keep in mind as you are getting ready to prepare for the MCAT and how the MCAT score directly connects to the admissions process.

- **Understanding Minimum Thresholds**—It's important that you do your homework to make sure you know what the various minimum MCAT thresholds are in order to know where you stand related to possible acceptance. First, do the homework. Go to each school's website and study up on what their minimum acceptable MCAT score is. The vast majority of schools will share this with you. Second, once you have the minimums, compare those with your own personal score.

- **Your Personal Score**—Once you have done your homework, compare the schools' minimum threshold scores with your own score. This does two things for you: 1) It provides you with a comparative list of how selective each school is related to their minimum admissions standards. 2) It shows you whether your current score is good enough to get into that particular school.

- **Create a List of Schools by Selectivity**—You should create a list featuring three types of schools:
  - **Tier One Schools**—These are the most competitive/ selective medical schools in the country. They have the highest science GPA and MCAT thresholds. For most students, these schools will form the most sought after and the hardest in which to get accepted.
  - **Tier Two Schools**—These are the schools that are the middle of the bell-curve in terms of their quality expectations and requirements. They will have middle of the road GPA and MCAT scores as their acceptance thresholds.
  - **Tier Three Schools**—These are the least competitive/ selective schools from a quality perspective. Most of these schools have the most flexible acceptance criteria. They tend to be newer schools whose primary concern is filling the seats.

Once you are finished making the list, compare your score with each tier. Where do you realistically land? Does your score fall in Tier 1, Tier 2, or Tier 3? This helps you to gain an understanding of where your MCAT puts you in terms of the type of school you should focus on. In other words, if you have a Tier 3 score, you shouldn't be applying to Tier 1 schools, as the likelihood of you being accepted is very low. But Tier 2 and Tier 3 schools are a better, more realistic bet for you. This is one of those moments in your search where you have to be honest with yourself about the type of school candidate you will be.

You can find good rankings of both allopathic and osteopathic universities on The Student Doctor Network. The rankings include a review of each school's average MCAT and GPA as well as feedback rankings from their interview day experiences and from feedback from thousands of students who shared both positive and negative feedback. This is all included in a Student Doctor Network Total Ranking. You can find this information at *www.studentdoctor.net* .

Prep Course vs. Studying on Your Own—I get this question a lot from a variety of medical student candidates. Should they study on their own for their MCAT preparation or take a prep course through a national provider. I am a believer in prep courses. They work. If you are a student who is great at self-motivation and discipline and can construct a study plan for MCAT preparation, then studying on your own may be a viable option. I also believe, however, it is a very small percentage of college students who can accomplish this.

If you are a student who struggles to be self-disciplined, a course forces you to become more disciplined about your studying and provides a very clearly outlined plan of content review that is easily followed.

Students should spend a minimum of six weeks studying every day to really prepare for the MCAT. A six-week study plan is what I recommend to students. But that is six weeks of non-stop preparation with no distractions. If you have to work or are taking classes while you prepare, plan to add weeks to that plan in order to make up for the time each day when you have to pay attention to other parts of life. Six weeks may turn into 10 weeks or more.

How Many Times Can You Take the MCAT?—According to the American Association of Medical Colleges (2020), the association which creates the MCAT exam, students can take the MCAT up to three times in a single year and up to seven times in a lifetime. The question I get a lot from students is how many times should they take the MCAT to get the best score possible.

The bottom line is this: It really shouldn't take you more than two or three attempts to get your best score. I have seen students take the MCAT five and six times and what I have seen is that after their second attempt, their score stays the same or actually decreases. Can you take the exam five times?

Yes. Does it impact how schools look at your scores? Yes, but: It can have a negative impact on the perception of your score when the school sees that you had to take the exam 4 times to get your best score.

I have sat in on hundreds of admission committee meetings in my professional lifetime and one of the topics that comes up frequently is how many MCAT attempts communicates that the student is an at-risk candidate. You just need to know that there is a perception that taking the exam four, five, or six times signals that you are not med school material. I would not waste your time, energy, and money by taking this exam four, five, six, or seven times.

CHAPTER 3

Applying to and Interviewing Successfully for Medical School

College students interested in attending need to begin the serious planning process at least 12 months prior to entering. I would suggest that the process actually needs to begin 20 to 22 months prior to your expected matriculation date.

I encourage students to begin thinking about their off-to-medical school preparations in November (22 months prior to start). This gives you 22 months to decide what schools to apply to and to prepare yourself and your family for what is a very significant change in your life. If you felt the transition to college was significant for you and your parents, this will be even more significant, by leaps and bounds.

Key Timeline for the Medical School Search Process

During the 22-month lead-up to your departure, there are a variety of key details you need to be focused on as you prepare. Whether you will be moving across the country or across the city, there are certain things you need to focus on in order to have the best preparation possible.

General Timeline:

November of Junior Yr.	May of Junior Yr.	July/August–After Senior Yr.
(Start Search Process)	(Begin Application)	(Matriculate Med School)

Junior/Senior Year Timeline—The last two years of undergrad are going to fly by for you. Not only will you be busy with academic work, you will also be engaged in social activities at your university. Plus, you will be planning on applying. Students who really have their world in order have an advantage over those who lack organization.

Here is what I would recommend you keep your eye on, as these key dates can help you stay on track:

List of Medical Schools—By the time you have reached **November of your junior year** of college, you need to be prepared to begin your search process. You should begin developing a long list of schools to which you want to apply and possibly visit. By the holiday period that December, you should have done your homework and scribbled out a long list of 20-25 schools. Get online and do your homework. Visit each school's website. Look at national ranking lists. Go to Student Doctor Network and look at feedback that students have left.

Shortlist of Medical Schools—By **February of your junior year** in college, you should have shortened that long-list of schools down to a shortlist of those to which you intend to apply. I recommend that final shortlist include no less than five and no more than 15 schools. This gives you the rest of the spring semester of your junior year to continue researching those on your shortlist. You want your final list solidified no later than April of your junior year.

May Launch of Application—Each **May**, the medical applications for both the allopathic and osteopathic world become available for the next year's entering classes. The application is a single application for all schools. The AMCAS (American Medical College Application Service) and the AACOMAS (American Association Colleges of Osteopathic Medicine Application Service) are separate services so for students wanting to apply to both types of schools, the process does require one to apply via the appropriate application. The application allows one to specify which schools to which you would like to send your application. Once you select the schools on the application and submit it, the application is automatically sent to each of the schools you specified.

It's very important that you understand that there are four timelines for applying to that are options for you. Please note the following:

- **Ideal Timing**—Applying between the **May application availability date and August 1**st. This gets your application in the queue at the very front and ensures that you will get an earlier decision which will help you guide other decisions that you will need to make. It also gives you the best chance to interview early in the fall semester, between September 1st and December 1st.

- **Moderately Ideal**—Applying between **August 2**nd **and November 1**st. This approach gets your application into schools during their fall semester. It means that you probably won't interview until after December 1st. That decision may have some risk associated with waiting that late to interview.

- **Less Than Ideal**—Applying between **November 2**nd **and January 31**st. By applying during this window, you are applying after most of the applicants will submit their applications. It also means that you may risk not being able to interview because most schools interview schedules will be full by mid-January.

- **Losing Option**—Application submission **after January 31**st is a losing option. There is very little chance of being offered a secondary application and even if you are offered a secondary, you will almost certainly not be offered an interview date, as all the slots for interviews have already been taken. My advice to those wishing to apply late in the cycle, after January 31st, is to wait until the next admission cycle and apply during the ideal time period.

Secondary Applications—Once each university reviews your primary application, they will be looking at key quantitative data points (MCAT and GPA) to ensure you meet their minimum requirements. They will also be checking to make sure all required application supporting documents have been received. Once this check is completed and you meet all minimum criteria, they will send you a secondary application asking for additional information. Typically, the secondary process includes additional essay questions, a criminal background check, and additional paperwork to be completed.

One of the additional documents required at this point in the process is the Health and Technical Standards document. This document outlines several health and psychosocial related criteria that the applicant must certify they can meet in order to become a medical student.

1) **Observation Standards**—Requires applicant to have proper sense of vision and somatic sensations.

2) **Communication Standards**—The applicant is required to be able to communicate fully including speech, hearing, reading, and writing.

3) **Sensory/Motor Skills**—This requires the applicant to be able to demonstrate gross motor and fine motor skills, be able to lift an approximate amount of weight, and be physically fit enough to stand for long periods of time.

4) **Conceptual, Integrative, and Quantitative Abilities**—Medical students must be able to stand and concentrate for long periods of time, including surgery, trauma, emergency room care, and other doctor/patient settings.

5) **Behaviors and Social Attributes**—Medical students must have the ability to demonstrate compassion, integrity, interpersonal skills, and personal qualities that will be assessed as part of their medical school career. (Kansas City University, 2020)

You must be able to meet these criteria and clearly demonstrate that you can do them on a regular basis. You are asked to sign a document confirming so.

Interviews and Medical School Visits—Interviews occur once the secondary application has been submitted. Most universities now have online schedulers which allow students to go online to schedule an available date for their interview. The process of scheduling has become very efficient. There are usually a finite number of interview dates and spots for each interview. My advice is to interview early and ensure you have a place at each school that offers you an opportunity to interview.

I will share more details and advice on how to complete a positive interview in later pages. One thing to keep in mind about the interview, however, is that this really is an opportunity for you to visit and see it up close and personal during your time there. Take advantage of this opportunity and make sure you ask questions.

Decision Time—By the time you have done your research, made your long list of schools, shortened that list to the final schools, submitted your applications, and interviewed, you will be a mini-expert on the med school world. It also means that you will need to bring yourself to a decision on where you ultimately want to attend.

By the end of February of your senior year, you should have acceptances; although these can arrive as early as October and come your way on a running basis, so don't expect them all at once. Once you have been accepted, it really is time to decide. You should be making your final decision in the month of April of your senior year, with the goal of notifying your school of choice no later than May 1st of your senior year.

Required Paperwork and Credentials—Once you have notified your school of choice, you will receive an email/

letter stating that you need to provide additional documents by a specified date. Be very careful with this one. When they state they want all the documents by the specified date, they mean it. Usually the documents include confirmation of vaccinations, finalized transcripts from your undergraduate institution, and a few other housekeeping items. Make sure you get these turned in on-time.

Picking the Right Medical School: Criteria for Narrowing Your List of Schools

Now that you know the right timeframe for you to make your choice within, it might not hurt to better understand the correct way to choose a college/university and the conversations and questions you need to be asking yourself as you begin the search. Knowing the general criteria that all students sift through in making one's decision is a good first step.

Criteria for Choosing a Medical School—As you begin the search process, there is a set of general criteria you must sort through in order to choose the university that best fits your personality, academic expectations, and general needs. I would suggest that you sit down at the beginning of your search process and go over the following variables to begin narrowing down your search. Then sit down again about halfway through your search process to get a sense of how your reaction to the criteria have changed as you have applied to, visited, and learned more about each school.

Allopathic v. Osteopathic—We have already discussed this at length in terms of differences, and the bottom line is that the differences are minimal. For some students, the approach to medicine is a prioritized criterion that matters a lot. As I stated in the last chapter, I would encourage you to consider applying to both types of schools.

Campus Safety—This is an important variable that doesn't get enough attention. How safe is the campus that you are visiting or attending? College/university campuses continue to spend more and more on campus safety and security related resources. This is driven by the market. Both students and parents want to ensure that they choose a college/university that is truly safe and secure.

With an increase in the number of on-campus sexual assaults, universities are under pressure to track and respond to such issues. The Jeanne Clery Act of 1990 requires all colleges and universities to self-report all crimes that occur on-campus property annually. They are required to post the report on their public website for both parents and students to review. I highly encourage all students to examine the campus crime statistics for each year. This will give you a more in-depth lens into their campus safety operation as well as an idea of the crimes that have occurred on-campus during that particular year.

Feeling safe, no matter where you go, matters. Medical students have enough on their minds already. You don't need to be worrying about the overall safety of your campus in addition to the stress you are under in class.

Diversity of the Student Body—For many students, the diversity of the student body is an important variable in their decision-making process, especially for students who are underrepresented minorities. These students want to know that they/you are attending a university where there is a critical mass of students who look like them/you.

Diversity encompasses all the ways we differ, so it includes a lot of variables: race/ethnicity, geography, religious beliefs, socioeconomic levels, sexual orientation, first-generation college students, etc. There are, therefore, a lot of aspects to diversity that can become a part of any student's search process. Don't be afraid to ask questions about the diversity on-campus. Med school admission offices are used to getting these questions and should have a lot of data to share with you about the level of diversity on-campus.

Be aware that the national average of underrepresented minorities on medical school campuses is around 13%-15% (Healthcareers.com, 2018). Therefore, you will definitely want to see where each university you are considering stands compared to the national average. In addition, med schools offer significant financial awards for under-represented minority students. Know that this may be an option worth exploring.

For-Profit v. Non-Profit—Up until 2010, there were virtually no for-profit medical schools in the country. In the last ten years, several for-profit institutions have been built. Given that the average private tuition is about $50,000/year, owning or investing in a medical school can produce substantial revenue. A class of 150 medical students can generate $7.5 million per year in revenue.

What students do not typically see is how much of that revenue is re-invested back into the actual programs and services of the school. What I have observed is that for-profit medical schools are primarily focused on maximizing revenue back to the owners/investors. That is the top priority before anything else is considered. Non-profit universities are missionally bound to reinvest any profits back into the educational programs and services that they offer to students.

If you are considering a for-profit med school as an option, do so with eyes wide open about the quality and quantity of services provided to students as well as how profits are managed and directed at the end of each academic and fiscal year. It is better to know than to not ask any questions and be surprised later.

Housing Options and Campus Amenities—Is it important that you live on-campus? What is medical student housing like? What additional amenities do you have access to on-campus (workout facility, coffee shop, campus bookstore, rock climbing gym, etc.)? There has been an on-going competition among colleges/universities to provide upgraded amenities for students for the last 20 years. This move has developed into an expensive building environment but has created many more opportunities for students on-campus. You will have to judge whether those amenities offered are important enough to sway your choice as you select your school.

Housing for graduate students is a real decision you will have to consider and make. For some students, being on-campus means being close to all the services, amenities, and academic resources they need to be successful. For other medical students, living off-campus provides them with some distance from campus that is a healthy boundary so that they do not spend 24/7 in the same physical location. Each student has their own preference.

Licensing Exam Pass Rates—How a school's graduates perform on the national licensing exams matters. It is a direct reflection of how the university's curriculum performs through each student taking the exam.

In order to be a licensed physician who can legally practice medicine, one must pass each level of the national licensing exam. There are two licensing exams: 1) The United States Medical Licensing Exam (USMLE), which is primarily, but not exclusively, taken by allopathic medical students. There are two levels of USMLE which each student must pass in order to graduate. 2) The Comprehensive Osteopathic Medical Licensing Exam (COMLEX) is the osteopathic version of the licensing exam, taken almost exclusively by osteopathic students. There are three levels of the exam which each student must pass in order to graduate.

Generally speaking, you will want to pay attention to how a particular school's average pass rate is either above or below the national average pass rate for the particular exam. Medical schools, whose students score above the national average, are generally in good shape. Schools whose scores are below the national average for the same exam are schools that are underperforming. Therefore, you would want to pay close attention to why, and to ask the school's admissions office why they are scoring below the national average.

Licensing exam pass rates should not be the only criterion you should consider. They form a piece to a much larger puzzle in the selection process. But they are a good indicator of the quality and effectiveness of the school's curriculum in preparing students for academic success.

Location (Rural vs. Suburban vs. Urban)—Location matters to students; this is one of those criteria that students talk a lot about, similar to size. Some want to attend a school in a more rural location because they like the idea of a place that sits alone and also are interested in ultimately practicing medicine in a similar location. More schools are being constructed in rural and underserved areas within the United States because of the need to graduate physicians in those geographic areas with the hope that they will stay and practice medicine.

Others may want to go to school right in the midst of a large city. They like the energy of an urban campus. They also have a desire to practice medicine within a city. Still others might want to attend in a suburban environment, as it provides the best of both worlds. There are some compelling reasons underscoring the importance of the location and how that impacts a student's experience.

- The location can impact one's eventual practice of medicine. Some students attend a medical school in a location where they did not initially think they would like to practice medicine in but they determine that the location is one where they enjoy living. I see this frequently in Kansas City where I work. Students come to campus from all over the United States, get to know the Midwest and Kansas City and realize that they want to stay and build both a career and a family in the area.

- The experience is more than classes, it is also about doing things in the surrounding community; sports, cultural events, concerts, museums, service projects, restaurants, and bars are all located within certain areas. Students don't just go to class; they also do things within the area they are located.

- The location can have an impact on personal finances. If a student chooses to go to school in a city which is in an expensive area, this can have a considerable impact on one's personal finances.

- Medical school location impacts how one travels. Transportation is an issue for any 22-26-year-old. For some, choosing a city location allows them to use public transportation (subway, train, buses) to navigate their way around the city, as well as to and from classes.

- Location can expose you to a variety of cultural experiences. For students in urban settings, they are exposed to all of those cultural experiences unique to American cities. For students who choose a rural setting, students are exposed to the experiences that are unique to those communities.

- Access to networking is key to students' CV development, career placement, and success. The location connects students directly to the physician/medicine networking that occurs within that particular community.

There is a best-fit campus for you and the location does help define what best fit is for you. Think it through.

Public v. Private—Private and public universities with medical schools tend to have their own personalities. Public universities are funded using taxpayer dollars to fund the school, whereas private universities are funded through private fundraising, tuition, and fees. Public universities, on average, tend to be larger than private schools in terms of total student enrollment, but that doesn't necessarily mean that their medical school is larger than private schools.

Public universities are required by law to not show favoritism towards a religious affiliation, consistent with constitutional limits, whereas private colleges can affiliate with a religious group and promote a particular religious viewpoint as part of their curriculum. How does this impact a school's curriculum? For example, there is a med school attached to a well-known, evangelical Christian university in Virginia. At that school, one would not be taught anything about abortion procedures as part of their OB/GYN curriculum; whereas students at other, non-religious affiliated schools would learn about abortion as part of the normal curriculum.

Both public and private colleges/universities are considered to have federal non-profit status, so they do not have to pay taxes based upon their revenues.

You, as the student, would have to determine whether this is a criterion for selection that matters to you. For some students, it matters. For others, it does not.

Quality and Reputation—Do rankings, prestige, and reputation matter in selecting a medical school? Yes and no. Ultimately it depends on the type of student you have been in undergrad and how you have performed on your MCAT exam. For 75% of students, getting accepted into one of the top schools in the country is not a possibility. I would suggest that prestige does not really matter for that 75% group.

For the top 25% of applicants, rankings, reputation, and prestige does matter and may play a role in the selection process. I would suggest you should do your homework and pay attention to the rankings, as you have a more realistic shot of getting into these top tier schools.

There are many metrics that communicate the quality and reputation of a particular medical school: Average MCAT score, average undergraduate cumulative GPA, average cumulative science GPA, reputation indicators in national rankings, and the selectivity of the university are all metrics that are used to communicate the reputation and quality of an educational institution.

There are big benefits to universities growing their reputation and quality metrics of their entering classes. The institutions are able to use those metrics for strategic planning purposes and in applying for the national rankings done by so many online outlets/magazines. They gain competitive advantages over their competition by being successful in the rankings game. I will warn you that the national rankings are exactly that, a game. The magazines and organizations that sponsor them play colleges/universities against one another in an effort to increase competitive advantages gained by increases in ranking profiles. If you are going to use the rankings as a tool for your search, I encourage you to pay close attention to the details within the rankings so that you make sure you are comparing apples to apples.

You will gain your own sense for the type of place you are interested in and what reputational variables are most important. Have a conversation with yourself about what matters to you as well as what doesn't. That helps to clarify your own mindset so that you will be clear about your priorities.

Research Prioritized—Offering medical students the chance to participate in research while they are learning to be physicians is a relatively new initiative supported by the accrediting bodies for medical schools. From a future looking perspective, having physicians who are able to complete research while practicing medicine is an important prospect for the profession and for medicine in general.

There are many students who are applying who have already done research, as undergraduates, during their science curriculum. Many of these students may wish to continue doing research as part of their experience. If you are one of those students, interested in research, you will want to ask the following questions as part of your search process:

- What percentage of medical students at a particular school actively participate in research?
- What is the total number of students participating in research?
- How much, budgetarily, does the university and/or med school commit to medical research?

Residency Placement Rates—According to the American Association of Medical Colleges and the American Association of Colleges of Osteopathic Medicine, there are approximately 26,000 graduates annually. This means that competition is stiff for placement in residency. These 26,000 graduates are competing for the open positions in residency programs all over the United States.

One pertinent indicator of school health and success is how many of their graduates are placed in residency positions post-graduation. In order to pay attention to this indicator of success, you should be looking at and demanding to see the following data points:

- Percentage of graduates, each year, that were placed in residency.
- What specialty was each student placed in for residency?
- What residency program each student was placed in as part of their residency match.

Retention and Graduation Rates—Twenty years ago, very few parents and/or students asked me about retention rates.

Now more and more students are asking the question, since it represents an important indicator of the school's health. A healthy school is able to keep its students they wish to retain throughout the four-year curriculum. Likewise, an unhealthy med school loses students.

The way in which they are measured on retention rates is by measuring the number of students who started in year one of med school and returned to start year two. In a study published by BMC Medical Education, the national average for medical student retention, over a ten-year period, is 94.3%. Understanding how many first-year medical students enter medical education, complete their first year, and then return for their second year is a metric which should be examined and questioned.

Similarly, graduation rates are an indicator of healthy or unhealthy schools. These are additional metrics worth looking at for each of the schools you are considering. Graduation rates track retention statistics for the first, second, third, fourth, fifth, and sixth years of school. Medical universities are required to report the percentage of students who entered during the first year that graduated in the fourth year and the sixth year. Such information tells an interesting story. According to the AAMC, the average graduation rate for medical schools is around 83% within the four-year time period.

It used to be that the vast majority of students attending, in America, graduated in four years. Now that number is changing as it is taking students longer to graduate from med school. Either metric tells a story, one you and your family may wish to consider carefully. The longer it takes to earn a degree, the more expensive that degree will be in terms of the overall cost.

Size of Medical School/University—Size does matter when it comes to colleges and universities, and medical schools. College/University student bodies may range from as few as 500 students to over 60,000 in the United States. Medical schools range in size from as small as 162 total students to as many as 2300 students on the large end of the spectrum. For many students, size hits at the heart of their decision as to what type of school they will ultimately choose. Some students want a smaller, more intimate experience, where they will know most of their fellow students and faculty on-campus, while other students are pulled towards a larger school. There are pros and cons to both options.

Some of the benefits associated with large medical schools are:

- Larger number of elective courses that aren't included in the core curriculum. These courses can complement and enhance students' experiences. Such courses might include bioethics, bioinformatics, research-based courses, and international medicine experiences.
- Larger universities often have housing options for medical students.

- Wide range of student activity options.
- State-of-the-art research facilities.
- Usually a high level of reputation within the state where they reside.

Some of the positive attributes associated with small schools are:

- Small class sizes, opportunities to know one's professors.
- Effective advising program where the advisers know their students well.
- Compelling sense of community.

This is an important conversation to have with yourself as you begin your search process. We have covered a lot of ground when it comes to the variables that you need to consider as part of the search process. There are many considerations, and you have to decide which to prioritize as part of your own consideration. Honestly, there is no right or wrong group of variables from which to choose. What matters is that you have: 1) taken the time to think them through; 2) decided which criteria are most important as a part of your decision; 3) weighed those criteria as you have visited and interviewed at campuses, and 4) used them to articulate why you are choosing the school(s) that you have selected. If you can follow that simple process, then your decision will more than likely be a good one.

Key Factors for Medical Students to Consider During Their Selection Process

You, as the prospective student, have an incredibly important role during the selection process. You have made it this far and are on the brink of the next steps in the selection process. Here are a few pieces of advice on how you can stay engaged in the process:

1) **It Requires Homework**—You are going to have to do your homework. You are used to homework, but you need to treat this process of looking into various schools seriously. There are great resources out there. First, they will send you marketing materials in the mail and via email. Collect it all so that you can look over what has been sent. Second, go on the school's website and dig around. There should be a page dedicated to both students and parents, and a page highlighting what is unique about their programs, but don't just limit your investigation there. Try to get a sense of what the place is like.

2) **Visit Campus**—This is important. Take notes. Bring up your thoughts, questions, and concerns with the faculty and staff who are made available to you during the visit. They should be able to answer your questions. Again, take notes so that you can reference them later.

3) **Ask Key Questions of Yourself**—The list of criteria for choosing a college/university are designed to breed questions. What size school do you feel most comfortable

attending? Do you prefer having the campus located in a city or somewhere less crowded? These are a couple of examples, but the sky is the limit. This may feel a bit awkward in the beginning but challenging yourself to justify why you are interested in a particular school is an important part of the self-reflection process.

4) **Set and Communicate a Deadline**—From the very beginning of the med school search process, you should set a date by which you have made your decision(s). Let's say that date is April 15th of your senior year. Throughout the process, you should keep reminding yourself that April 15th is the deadline. And you need to hold yourself to that target.

You will eventually reach the point where you have made your decision and you will know where you wish to enroll. That is an exciting reality. It also allows you to move forward with preparing yourself to go off to school in a matter of months. Your conversations with your family and yourself will now begin to shift from "What do you like about that medical school?" to something more about what you are looking forward to when you visualize yourself on the actual campus. The transition has begun.

Preparing for a Medical School Interview

By this point, you have successfully narrowed down the schools to which you wish to apply. You have submitted your application and you made it through the first round of the selection process. You have completed the secondary application. And finally, you have been invited to campus for an interview.

This means that the office of admission has first reviewed the quantitative factors of their admissions process. The three key quantitative data points they are reviewing are your cumulative GPA from your undergraduate institution, your cumulative science GPA from undergrad, and your MCAT score. Once they have reviewed these quantitative factors first, then they move on to reviewing the qualitative factors of your application material and this is where the interview plays a very important role.

What do you need to do to ensure that you have a successful interview? This is the critical, final step in the selection process. The good news is that it allows the school to meet you and get to know you; and equally important for you to get to know the school. In all honesty, it is really yours to screw up, as the interview is really designed to identify outliers; those students who are either extraordinary or not qualified at all to attend med school. For the vast majority of interviewees, it is a process they will get through unscathed and be accepted by the University. For the school, it is the most important qualitative factor in assessing your performance as an applicant. The following is a list of qualitative factors that a university evaluates candidates on in order of importance:

1) *Interview Performance*
2) Graduate vs. Undergraduate Degree (Where from and quality of degree)

3) Personal Background/Behavior
4) Personal Statement
5) Letters of Recommendation
6) Interactions with the University
7) Recent Community Service
8) Work History
9) Shadowing Opportunities with Physicians

Notice that the interview performance was the top, and most critical, factor for evaluation. The bottom line is that the process is important to you getting in. My hope is to provide you with advice that will ensure you navigate this final step successfully.

What advice do I have for applicants? The following general advice is for your consideration:

Be Prepared—Do your homework on each school you visit for an interview. Showing up and winging it won't do and is an obvious negative for you. As part of your homework, develop a set of questions that you want to ask students, faculty, and staff. Don't ask the obvious questions, just for the sake of asking a question. For example, if you know basic information, ask a higher-level question. Instead of asking what their board scores are for their second-year class, ask, "I know you have high board scores, to what do you attribute that success?"

Be Professional—Show up and demonstrate to them that you can be a part of this profession. Dress appropriately, as if you are a physician seeing patients in an office (I.e. professional dress). Act like the physician you wish to become…act like you are a physician in terms of the way you carry yourself. Demonstrate courteousness and graciousness.

Be Articulate, Yet Concise—Express yourself fluently and coherently. But don't ramble. This is not a time for you to tell hour long stories to your friends. This is, in essence, a job interview. In fact, the interview may actually be designed to give you multiple mini interviews where you have to concisely answer questions in a very short period of time. If English is not your first language, take time to work with a professional who can assist you in preparing for your interview.

Be Aware That You are Being Evaluated—From the moment you arrive on-campus for your interview, to the moment you leave, you should assume you are being evaluated. Most assuredly, that means in the actual interview; but you are also being evaluated as well when you are not in the interview. Many schools will pair an interviewee or group of interviewees up with a current student for a campus tour. Assume that all of your interactions with your fellow interviewees and the student tour guide are being evaluated.

Be Confident—You have earned your spot for that particular interview day. Act like it. But don't be cocky. Demonstrate a reserved confidence. Don't act like you know everything. If you are an introvert who struggles to convey confidence and strength, take time during undergrad to work with someone who specializes in helping introverts to prepare for public events such as your interview. Someone in your university's communication department might be a good starting point.

Be You—Don't fake it to make it. Be your genuine self during the interview process. You will be perceived as more genuine and authentic if you just be yourself.

Questions You May Be Asked During a Medical School Interview

1) **Why do you want to be a Doctor?** This goes back to the process you began in undergrad when you decided to apply. This should be an easy question to answer as it is something you have already given a lot of thought to.

2) **What about you would make you a good doctor?** Think about your strengths and weaknesses, what makes you passionate about medicine, and what drives you as an individual. All of this should be part of your answer.

3) **How do you handle stress?** Being a physician is a stressful job. Have you thought about this? If not, consider it and think about not only how you handle stress now, but how you will handle stress in med school and residency, as well.

4) **Why Allopathic/Osteopathic Medicine?** The schools want to know that you have given thought to the foundational philosophies behind why they exist. This is a question that

students get tripped up on very regularly. Simply saying, "I want to be a MD because I want to be a doctor…" won't cut it. Know the history of both allopathic and osteopathic medicine; be able to articulate those philosophies and why you see yourself as an MD or DO.

5) **Why the Specific Medical School?** Remember, you need to do your homework on any school that has invited you to interview. Know the history, values, curricular details, etc. and be prepared to answer this question.

6) **Describe your research experience.** If you have research experience, share it! If you lack research experience, use this as a transition to a conversation about why you are picking this school and want to be involved in the specific research being offered at that school.

7) **Describe your work experience and how it informs your decision to go to medical school.** Have you been out of college for a while and your application highlights your work experience? If so, this is a question you are likely to get during the interview. Be prepared to share how your work experience informed your decision.

8) **Presented with an ethical dilemma.** Many universities are moving towards presenting applicants with a bioethics-based dilemma and are asking students to articulate both sides of an ethical argument. For example, they might ask you to explain how you would articulate the necessity/lack

of necessity for the COVID 19 quarantining of millions of people from a public health perspective. This is less about what your personal belief is about the topic but more about whether you can articulate two sides of the argument.

9) **Assessment of teamwork.** Many schools are including some team exercise as part of their interview process. Be prepared to work with a team of interviewees to solve some kind of problem. You will be evaluated on the kind of team member you were. You may also be asked specifically what kind of team member you are, so be prepared to accurately reflect on the type you perceive yourself to be. You may even use an example from your life when you were a member of a team as a way to illustrate your teamwork abilities.

10) **Tell me your personal story.** This requires you to talk about your background. Think about the pertinent parts of your life that you would highlight for a stranger who is evaluating you. You want to create an impression. Most of us think our own personal story is boring. You don't want to approach this question with that attitude.

11) **Strengths and weaknesses.** The common mistake is to have a laundry list of strengths, but no weaknesses. You definitely want to highlight your strengths, but you want to also include some weaknesses. Use your weakness to pivot your answer to something that the process can help you turn into a strength!

12) **What questions do you have?** Remember that your homework on each school should have created a list of high-level questions that you have developed. You want to have a question or two for your interviewer. Don't get to the end and say, "I don't have any questions..." That will cost you in terms of the interviewer's evaluation.

Practice makes perfect when it comes to interviews. If your undergraduate institution offers a pre-med committee mock interview, take part in it. Any practice you can get to simulate your interview, will be beneficial.

CHAPTER 4

Getting Ready to Go:
Preparing for Life to Change

Look how far down the road you are to heading off to medical school. Really think about all you have accomplished so far. It is pretty amazing to think about all you have done to get to this moment: consider your applications, secondary applications, your interview, and med school visits, as you have accomplished so much.

What awaits you around the corner? One of the most challenging experiences of your life will become part of your life before you know it, but you still have a few things to think about, a few questions to answer for yourself, and a few important things to do in order to be ready to go off to your first day.

Key Questions and Conversations Regarding What to Expect at Medical School

Now that you have decided where you are going to med school and are actually enrolled, a new phase of your work begins. In order to have yourself in tip-top shape emotionally and mentally, you really need to begin to talk to yourself. No, my goal isn't to get you declared mentally incompetent, my goal is to get you thinking about some key questions that assist you in becoming mentally prepared for your med school experience. The following are a few to get a self-conversation started:

1) What about med school makes you nervous?

2) What are you most excited about when you think of going off to med school?

3) What parts of the med school experience will come easiest to you?

4) What parts of the experience will come hardest to you?

5) When you think about getting to the end of this, what do you see?

Don't be afraid to think about the future. I can promise you will learn something about yourself that you did not know before you started considering these issues. And the bottom line is that you will become even more connected with yourself than anyone else in this world. Being able to listen to your inner voice, knowing your strengths and weaknesses, and being honest with yourself will benefit you greatly. Don't be nervous to think about these important self-conversations about the following issues you will certainly confront during your four years in medical training:

Academic Accommodations—According to a study conducted by the University of Michigan, approximately 5% of students going to med school receive some kind of academic related accommodations for a physical or learning disability. It is a very common thing. If you have a physical and/or learning disability and have received some kind of academic or physical accommodations during some or all of K-12 and/or college, you should request the same or similar accommodations for your time in med school. Be aware that you are going to ask for help, though. First, you need to sit down and review the accommodation process. Second, pull together all of your paperwork and documentation from K-12 and/or college, as it will be needed. Third, you will need to fill out an application for accommodations *BEFORE* you arrive, and you will need the documentation to help you complete the application. Follow the instructions on the application to the tee, as most institutions will require it and will decline your request if you don't provide exactly what is requested.

One of the biggest mistakes medical students make is not requesting academic accommodations before they arrive. I have seen it occur time and time again. Don't be prideful about this. If you needed the accommodations then, you probably need them now. Remember: the school cannot be expected to read your mind.

Drugs and Alcohol—You are choosing a career which is antithetical to being impaired while professionally practicing. In fact, it's against the law to practice as an impaired physician. Yet 15% of physicians are addicted to drugs and/or alcohol. So simply being a doctor does not make you immune to the lure of drugs, alcohol, and overall substance abuse.

In a recent study conducted by the University of Florida, it was discovered that 25% of medical students admitted using marijuana during school. Regardless of state laws allowing the personal/casual use of marijuana (states such as Colorado, Washington, and California), physicians and medical students who are practicing medicine are legally liable for being under the influence of marijuana even if the state they are practicing in allows casual use.

Marijuana is not the only drug being used by medical students. Forty-six percent of students from the nine medical schools in Florida admitted that their prescription drug use increased during med school. Sixty-four percent of those students surveyed admitted that the prescription drugs they ingested did not belong to them.

Concerns about drug use among medical students also exist. Illicit and illegal drugs are always a concern. The most prevalent overuse of drugs among medical students is over the usage of unprescribed stimulants such as Adderall, Vyvanse, or Ritalin. Students believe they can focus better when they are on these stimulants. They usually procure them from a friend. If caught, they risk being dismissed.

According to a study conducted by University of Florida, approximately 70% of medical students admit to binge drinking. Based upon my own professional experience, I would estimate that the number is actually higher than the reported number given that many students don't admit to engaging in such behavior.

Binge drinking has been the number one health issue for undergraduate and graduate students dating back almost 35 years. Over 1800 college students, 18-24 years old, have died in the last year from alcohol related accidents and incidents. Twenty-five percent of students indicated that their academic standing and grades are directly impacted negatively by their drinking. Binge drinking has both health and academic consequences.

There is no sign that this trend will disappear any time soon. Just because you are a doctor in training, does not make you immune to the effects of excessive drinking. I had a recent third year medical student, whose performance on clinical rotations began to slip. I scheduled a time to talk to him and, after poking and prodding around the root issue of his academic slippage, he admitted to me that he believed he had a drinking problem. I immediately referred him to our state physician's health program. They worked with him and offered support, an opportunity to work on his sobriety. He has since graduated and is a physician who now speaks to medical students about his own experience with alcohol and the value of the physician's health program…and personal sobriety.

If you or your classmates are struggling with alcohol, illicit drug use, or are using unprescribed medications and need help, reach out to the Office of Student Affairs at your university. They are trained to help refer you on to professionals who can help you. If you are proactive and reach out to them, there is no chance of your being in trouble.

Sex—It happens. I know this isn't an easy conversation to have. My own dad sat silently and awkwardly, while my mom had "*the Talk*" with me (we still laugh about it today). For many medical students, sex must be considered a critical issue that has real consequences. Sexual assault is a very real thing on college campuses, and medical schools and med students are not immune either. Men need to understand the risks they take on when engaging in sexual activity. Words like "consent", "inebriation", "no means no", and "rape" are actual parts of the college and medical school lexicon. Women need to understand the risks that are prevalent in alcohol-centric social environments. These are all part of the complicated layers of sexual behavior on and off university campuses. Most schools are talking about general wellness on their campuses and sexual wellness includes ensuring that the community is free of rape and sexual assault. Regardless of your gender, this is an issue where medical education needs both men and women supporting efforts to stem this tide.

Sexual Orientation—Approximately 5% of students identify as LGBTQIA (Lesbian, Gay, Bisexual, Transgender, Queer/

Questioning, Intersex, and Asexual) during their undergraduate years. We know from national research that 5% is a low number because many students won't share their orientation or identity for fear of discrimination (Nama, MacPherson, Samson, and McMillan, 2017).

Higher education administrators within medical education realize that somewhere between 5% and 15% of their student body must be LGBTQIA. Having been an administrator at both undergraduate and graduate institutions, I have found anecdotally that more than 5% of our students within the med school are out publicly, but there remain a percentage of students who remain closeted because of the same fears of discrimination.

National research supports this reality within med schools. A 2015 study by the Stanford University School of Medicine found that 40% of the medical students identifying as "Not Heterosexual" were afraid of discrimination. Additionally, 30% of those medical students choose not to disclose their sexual orientation/identity because of a fear of discrimination.

A recent medical school first year class had 4 transgender students in it, 3 of which asked to have their status remain confidential, which was honored by the university. This was our largest number of transgender students in one class that I personally had experienced in my professional career. But it signals not only a shift in the numbers of LGBTQ students coming into medical school, it also highlights the need for med schools to be ready to teach our medical students about LGBTQ health within our curricula.

I want to be upfront with you if you are a LGBTQAI student. Bias about sexual orientation exists at med schools, just as it does in the greater community. And a very high percentage of medical students choose to remain closeted because of this bias, real or perceived, that might impact their professional trajectory. I understand this concern. But we need to strive to be ever better when it comes to supporting all students, regardless of their sexual orientation and preferences. I always promote non-judgment and unconditional love as the foundation for any discussions I have with students about these issues.

Lastly, there is a national push for med schools to step up to the plate and add LGBTQAI health initiatives as a part of the curricula. This has been embraced by some schools, while others are slow to make the change. Students can play a major role in promoting change to the curriculum at their particular school. Who wants to take this on as their personal pet project?

Personal Safety—I know it seems a little counter-intuitive to be sitting down to talk with you about personal well-being and safety when you are essentially entrusting your safety and well-being to the college/university to which you are going. I get it. First, when you pay tuition you are expecting that institution to provide reasonable safety and security for you. And consequently, the university is on the hook for insuring your well-being. Colleges and universities spend millions and millions of dollars, each year, on campus safety and security operations.

From an insider's perspective, I can assure you that the university takes this part of their mission very seriously. That being said, don't take your personal safety in med school for granted. Remember that common sense rules the day in the following ways: 1) never walk alone on-campus after dark; 2) having a "buddy" that you arrive and leave with from every social event with; 3) lock your apartment/house/residence hall room door when you leave for the day, and; 4) making sure you know how to contact campus security in case of an emergency.

Financial Expectations—Most medical students have a foundation of financial freedom and planning by the time they reach graduate school. After all, most of you have been living on your own at least for the four years of college, some even longer. That independence extends further. And if you are depending upon your twice-yearly financial aid student loans for survival exclusively, your financial responsibility is more important than ever before. According to the U.S. Department of Education, approximately 76% of medical students pay for medical school using federal financial aid programs to fund the experience, including tuition, fees, and living expenses. What details should you consider?

- **Bank Account**—You need a checking account with a debit card from a bank that is physically close to your school. This may require you to change banks in the event you change cities.

You should also be prepared to provide your bank account number and your bank's routing number to both the Office of Financial Aid and your University's Business or Finance Office. They will want to transfer funds into your bank account electronically and will need this information to do that. The importance to you about this critical request is that this is the way the Feds will deposit your financial aid loan disbursement into your account. If it is about your continued day-to-day survival, it is important.

- **Monthly Budget**—Fixed income. Get used to saying that uncomfortable phrase. If you are depending upon federal financial aid for your living expenses, the importance of maintaining a monthly budget is critical to staying financially solvent. Because you only receive financial aid disbursement twice per year, it will require you to not overspend month-to-month. If you do overspend, there is no surplus or cushion from which to draw.

  You will want to track your finances as closely as you track your day-to-day study plan for your courses.

- **To Work or Not to Work**—I will be very direct about this one. There is no way you can hold down a part-time or full-time job and succeed in med school at the same time. Do I know anyone who has done this successfully? Yes. One student who was literally sleeping in the back of his car, worked the night shift at a local hospital, then went to class during the day. It was a torturous schedule and I have no idea how he pulled it off. All of the others who tried to both work and do med school simultaneously failed miserably. Don't try it. It is a waste of time, resources, and energy.

How to Solve Problems in Medical School—Medical school is very different from your undergrad, in that the university sees you as a professional in training, not a kid who is in college. Therefore, you are expected to solve problems on your own.

Problem solving is a life skill that hopefully you have developed by the time you have decided to become a physician. The responsibility is yours to solve those problems. Every year, I encounter a certain number of students who do not heed our advice about reaching out for help to solve issue(s). And in almost every case, after my staff and I have helped them to solve their issue, they say, "I wish I had taken advantage of this help sooner…"

The good news is that there are highly trained experts on-campus who are there to help you solve problems. During your orientation, you will meet a group of people from Student Services or Student Affairs whose job it is to help you solve problems. Pay attention to what they are saying in orientation, write down their names and contact information. Use them as resources.

Going Home—The verbiage "going home" is limited to the 20%-25% of medical students who are married and/or have kids. Going home each night is very different for you than your friends who are single and have no kids. When you go home in the evenings you have a spouse and possibly children who hold expectations for you. You will feel torn between your need to study and your need to spend time with the people you love.

I encourage you to come up with a "Going Home Routine" and do the same routine every night you are at the house with your family. You can determine what that routine is, but it might look something like the following:

- 5:30—Arrive Home
- 5:30-6 p.m.—Play with the kid(s)
- 6 p.m. to 7 p.m.—Family dinner time
- 7 p.m. to 8 p.m.—Study time
- 8 p.m.—Kids go to bed
- 9 p.m. to 10 p.m.—Study time
- 10 p.m. to 11 p.m.—Quiet time with spouse
- 11 p.m.—Bedtime

Self-Advocacy Skills—Students need to learn how to advocate for themselves, so they do not have to call either their parents or friends anytime they are confronted with either a problem or a difficult decision. For example, students who need academic-related accommodations, must complete the application prior to arriving for classes (otherwise the accommodations won't exist once classes begin).

Medical Student Checklist for Departure

I could spend a lot of time creating a laundry list of things that students need to take with them, but it would be obsolete the moment I publish this book. Instead, I would like to recommend you focus on seven important factors during the summer before you leave:

1) **Time to Celebrate**—Make sure you give yourself a limited amount of time to celebrate your big accomplishment of graduating from undergrad and being accepted to medical school. Spend time with friends. Sleep in a little. Have fun.

2) **Vacation with Family**—It is extremely important for your family—parents and siblings—to have one bit of time together prior to you leaving. That could be a weekend where everyone is home or a significant vacation somewhere you all want to go. Take the time to be together, because many families discover that once you are off at med school, there is much less time for family contact which can fit into your busy schedule.

3) **READ**—I know. This is this last thing you want to do before you go away to read professionally for two years straight. You don't have to read science texts, you just need to read. It can be People Magazine, The Catcher in the Rye, or the newspaper. As long as you

79

are reading every day and keep the rust from settling in your brain, you will be ok.

4) **Exercise Regularly**—Get in the mode of exercising every day. Make it a habit during the summer prior to med school so that you will make it a habit once you start classes.

5) **Last Outing with Friends**—I encourage you to identify your 1, 3, 5, 15 closest friends and have some kind of fun outing with that group. Once you go off to med school there is much less time for you to connect with your friends at home. This outing is a way to celebrate friendships as well as the accomplishments that have led to your post-college futures.

6) **Conversation with Family About How Life Will Be Different**—This is an important one. Life is about to change for you. And it is going to change for your family as well. As you dive into classes, you are going to have far less time to dedicate to family phone calls, text messages, events, traditions, etc. It is therefore critically important that you sit your family down, remind them that you love them, and then break the news to them that you will not have as much time for them as you have had in the past. Explain the demands of what you are going to go through. Share with them the number of hours each day you will be in class, in lab, at clinical sites, studying at home, and stress the

fact that your being organized about all of this means less time with family.

They may not like this change, but they will understand it to whatever level they can without going through it themselves. It may be necessary to remind them about this from time to time.

7) **Saying Thank You**—Gratitude is infectious, and when you express it to people you admire and are thankful for, you will reap the benefits. I, therefore, encourage you to write thank you notes to the people you believe helped you get to this point in your life. This could be grandparents, a teacher, a boss from a summer job, a coach, the doctor who let you shadow them, or family members. Regardless of who they are, I encourage you to make a thank you list and then write a note to each of those people to be sent immediately before you leave town. Saying thank you means a lot to the recipient and may pay both short- and long-term dividends once med school is completed. It's important to keep your cheerleaders cheering for you well into the future. Say thank you to the people who helped you reach this major point in life.

Before You Actually Move

Before you are wheels down in the city, one final bit of homework is required. As always, there are a few more important things you should take care of:

- **Family Contact/Friend**—Find out if your family has any contacts within the city where you will be living. Family friends can serve a variety of roles. They can be an emergency contact. They can serve an occasional home cooked meal for you. They can be a place where you can escape to in order to study.

    I had a student whose family friend was a cardiologist at a local hospital. When she failed her Cardiopulmonary System course, he stepped up and helped her successfully remediate the course.

- **Find a Physician**—You need to create a "healthcare home" in the city where you will be living. Going to urgent care anytime you are sick is not a recipe for good, consistent health. Do your homework and ask your school's Office of Student Affairs if they have a list of endorsed physicians to which students may be referred. The importance of this step is critical to maintaining any treatment plans you are already on, prior to arriving at school.

- **Find a Pharmacy**—Same thing. Do your homework and find a pharmacy near your apartment or house where you will be living while in med school.

- **Tech Tune-Up**—Make sure all of your technology is up to speed and working efficiently. I have seen many students show up to school with their 5-year-old laptop in tow: invariably, it dies the first week of classes. Take some time to update software and ensure that the hardware is working well before you land in town.

Once You Move In

There are just a few things I recommend you do once you are on the ground in your new location:

- **Warehouse Shopping**—Hit a Sam's Club or Costco equivalent to purchase those staples you will need every day but won't have time to go get once classes start.

- **Find Your Way**—Drive or walk around and get comfortable with where things located; Bank…check; Pharmacy…check; Doctor's office…check; The way to campus…check.

  If you live in a city that has great public transportation options, go for a ride and perform the same checklist.

- **Talk to the Locals**—Find a "local" whom you trust and ask them for directions to a favorite restaurant, coffee shop, or off-campus quiet spot that could be used for studying. You won't want to study or eat on-campus all the time. You need to get away periodically just to keep your sanity. The locals will know the best spots and would be happy to share them with you.

- **Settle into School Work**—Make sure whatever paperwork you were sent to help prepare for orientation is completed. Look over your orientation schedule. Go so far as to go to campus and familiarize yourself with the names of the buildings and where everything will be held for orientation. This is also the time when your mindset must change and your laser-like focus should be on med school. It is about to begin!

You are now just a matter of days away from both your first day and initial week. It's game time. Are you ready? Have you heeded the advice and prepared the way you should have? If you haven't, remember, use the student assistance resources at your school that are available to you. For now, dive headfirst into orientation and use that time to mentally prepare yourself for what is to come.

CHAPTER 5

The First Day of Medical School

There are very few moments in life where you truly can start over from square one and reinvent yourself. Going off to college, if you will recall, was one of those moments. Getting married, having a child, and going off to med school are others. Virtually no one knows who you are, what you are about, what type of student you were in undergrad, and they won't know about any of the skeletons in your proverbial closet. What a great opportunity!

As you start your first day, think about the parts of your life you would like to jettison and other new, and exciting pieces to your life in which to invest. Now I am not talking about changing your name and making up some elaborate story about who you are and where you are from. I am talking about letting go of the accumulated baggage you have been carrying along with you and learning from that baggage in a way that allows you to change old habits that have been hard to break. This is part of being emotionally, mentally, and physically prepared for your new life, for that is the type of opportunity you have in starting this new journey.

I have emphasized the importance of being prepared for med school, the need to have your brain and organizational skills in tip-top shape, as well as being prepared to be professional each and every day (you will read more about professionalism soon). What will that first day of orientation look like for you and, if they have accompanied you, your family? You can expect the day to look something like the following:

- **Early Morning Arrival**—You will be told when and where to arrive. Make sure to get there at least 30-45 minutes in advance of the start of the first orientation session, which will allow you some time to get to the location, meet some of your classmates, find a seat in the auditorium, and settle in. Showing up late is bad form and unprofessional.

- **Welcome from the President**—You are going to hear a message from the university's president. That message will include key parts of the university's values and mission that students will learn during the orientation process.

- **Key Leaders**—You are going to be introduced to key leaders. The Dean of your school will talk with you about what a great accomplishment it is to be accepted. He/she will also talk about his/her expectations for you as a student.

You will also be introduced to the experts, whose job it is to help you. Usually these are the Office of Student Services staff which covers student activities, learning enhancement, counseling services, tutoring, etc. Take notes and make sure you write down names and contact information for each of these people as you will need these resources.

- **Parents Meeting**—Typically, the school will have a parent specific session. While you are out taking a campus tour, your parent(s) will meet with university staff to talk about what it is like to be the parent of a medical student. The staff will share their collective wisdom with your parents on how to navigate supporting you during what will be a very difficult four-year process.

- **Rites of Passage**—Each university has their own traditions that welcome you into the family of that particular institution. These are usually meaningful traditions full of symbolism and a time to take pictures and celebrate your amazing accomplishments to this point. One that has become a tradition at most schools is a White Coating Ceremony. This is a ceremony that emphasizes your entrance into the world of medicine, and the

STRAIGHT TALK FOR MEDICAL STUDENTS

penultimate moment of the ceremony is when you are presented with your student physician's white coat.

- **Breaking Bread**—The university will have some kind of time to sit down as a family to have a meal on-campus.

- **Time with Your Family**—Most universities want to make sure that you do have time at the end of the first day to just be together as a family. This gives you the chance to have that last shopping trip to Target or Walmart or have a final meal together as a family, at a local restaurant. Take advantage of this time to do something as a family. It might just be quiet conversation in your new apartment or house or a big celebration with multiple family and friends. The main issue is that you do something together.

Programs and Services Designed to Support You in Medical School

Collectively, colleges and universities around the country spend untold millions of dollars on providing support services to their student bodies. More than ever before, higher education is being held responsible for being able to demonstrate the return on investment for the education they are providing to you. A swath of the American public has begun questioning the value of advanced education and, more specifically, what students get for the tuition that they pay.

There is a laundry list of services that colleges and universities provide for students. The larger the university, the more programs and services that are available to help students. That being said, at a minimum, you can expect that the following student support services will be available in one form or another:

Campus Ministry—Most colleges and universities have a campus ministry office that is ecumenical in nature. For public colleges/universities, there are ministry programs for all the major religions (Christian, Judaism, and Muslim). At private colleges and universities, most cater to Christian students, but also offer outreach for Jewish and Muslim students. At very conservative private universities, Christian religious ministries may be the only ministries that are offered. Regardless of the type of university you are attending these religious ministries are available to the undergraduate and the graduate populations. Don't be hesitant to use these services if you are needing this kind of support.

Regardless of one's belief structure, students' religious identity development is a key part of the four years of any college/med school experience.

Career Services—One of the most important Return on Investment (ROI) metrics for any university to demonstrate is whether you will get a job upon graduation. The area of career services and career counseling is a growing area on most campuses. In my experience, students who engage with career services early and consistently during their time in med school have a greater chance at residency placement.

Most med school career services offices offer students career exploration tools in medicine, resume/CV development, interview preparation, mentoring opportunities, and career placement following graduation. I highly encourage students to at least utilize the career exploration options as well as opportunities for internships.

Counseling Services—We have already touched on how important it is for students to maintain general wellness, which includes their personal mental health. All colleges and universities either provide direct counseling services on-campus or they contract with off-campus providers to cover the same issues. Colleges/universities have made access to these services as easy as possible, even removing a fee-for-service approach, by making free services available.

Most students take advantage of the on-campus resources, as they are, in many cases, close to academic classes. A small percentage of students don't want to be seen on-campus waiting for a counseling appointment. If you or a friend could use someone to talk to for whatever reason, I highly encourage you to reach out to Counseling Services or Student Services (who can then make them an appointment). It can be time well-spent.

Learning Enhancement—Ensuring that students are successful academically requires colleges and universities to provide learning enhancement services to all students. This includes one-on-one options to meet with a professional who specializes in aiding students to develop their study skills, providing a wide ranging/reaching tutoring program, and providing both assessment and testing services that benefit students who may have learning disabilities.

The error that some students make is assuming that tutoring is only available for those who need remedial help. Quite the contrary. My staff and I tracked internal data to look at what percentage of our medical students were using tutoring and professional study skills services. We found that over 75% of our medical students were getting supplementary academic support in any given year; the implication being that the very smartest and most accomplished students at the university were utilizing such services. I encourage you to avoid developing pre-disposed opinions about participating in a large or small group tutoring session, as the services are typically free, and some portion of your classmates will be present, as well. I can share a multitude of stories about how tutoring or working with a learning specialist took a student from struggling to successful in a matter of weeks.

A first-year medical student was struggling to develop the study skills she needed to be successful. She failed her first two medical school classes. Although she did not believe working with a learning specialist would work, we were able to convince her to spend one hour with one of the staff. They analyzed her study plan and came to the conclusion that all of it was pretty decent, with one glaring omission: she was only studying by herself. She did not like studying in a group of people. The learning specialist challenged her to find a study group and to study the week before her next exam doing a combination of both study time alone and then studying with a group. Studying with a group gave her a whole new perspective on how to look at the course material and she was able to talk out concepts which were difficult for her to understand. It worked. Her next exam, she received a B- grade, a substantial improvement over her previous failing grades.

Medical Services—The most sought-after service on university campuses are medical services. These types of services are extremely expensive to maintain. Usually larger colleges/universities can provide these, through a university health center, because they have a medical school and/or hospital associated with the institution, which helps to reduce overall cost. For smaller colleges, health services have become extremely expensive to maintain and so they look to create local partnerships that allow students reduced or free access to healthcare.

Students both demand and deserve quality health services while at college, because they often don't take the time to care for themselves: when they get sick, they want to get help closely and immediately. Make sure to ask questions about the type of medical services that the college/university provides. Although these services should be seen as supplementary to your health insurance, they are nonetheless important.

Mentoring Program—Most schools have a program in place for peer-to-peer orientation to the experience. Each campus titles their program differently, but the basic idea behind the concept is to pair a new student with a second, third, or fourth year medical student for mentoring. Peer-to-peer mentoring has its benefits. First, it provides you with an immediate student level relationship that you can turn to during the orientation process. Second, students tend to believe that other students have *street credibility*, whereas old administrators like myself may lack such credentials. Because your mentor possesses the street "cred", they can answer questions the administration cannot.

Most institutions have the mentors walk you through the orientation process, providing student-level advice, candor, and encouragement. The students chosen to mentor are effectively trained and will know the support resources that are available should the need arise.

Student Activities—Research by long-time higher education researcher Dr. George Kuh revealed that students who are engaged in two or more campus organizations, activities, and/or leadership roles, are more academically successful and generally happier with their college experience. This research extends to medical school as well.

I encourage you to be active in student organizations as the benefits may be great. All colleges and universities have opportunities for multi-faceted development of the student. Whether it is in a social organization, a leadership role in student government, or performing community service, there are many possibilities for involvement.

The university will provide a detailed outline of the activities that are available to students in their admission material, in their catalog and student handbook, and will provide some kind of "Activities Fair" for students to get to know what organizations are available. I encourage you to look at the list of activities before you arrive and then to seek out those activities in which you are most interested. Some of those key activities include, but are not limited to:

- College Union Activities
- Community Service
- Social Organizations
- Student Government or Student Senate
- Student Organizations Focused on Medicine

Advice for You on Day One of Orientation

What kind of advice do I share with students on day one of orientation? Some of it is lighthearted, some is congratulatory, some is sympathetic, some is direct and honest, some is advice that second, third, and fourth year students want me to give you, and some is just benign.

- **Don't Blow This Off**—The people who have designed and put together your orientation are not just standing up in front of a group of students because they like to hear the sound of their own voices. They are sharing real and valuable information about situations that can arise. What we are sharing with you is meant to lead to your success. If you blow the entire orientation off, it is your loss.

I have had students who spent the entire first day of orientation outside the building on their cell phones, because apparently their calls were more important than what was being shared in the sessions. Don't be that guy.

- **Take Notes**—Treat orientation like a class, before classes have started. Take notes, especially as it may pertain to key names, contact information, and processes that you will need to know in order to pull off your daily study and course schedule.

- **You Are Being Evaluated**—This is the one that most students are completely oblivious to: the entire time you are in orientation, you are being evaluated by the faculty and staff. If you fall asleep, if you are a jerk, if you are disrespectful to a classmate...all of this is noted.

I had a group of guys in orientation a few years ago who all fell asleep in the same row. I labeled them the "Narcoleptics" and even called them out during the session, thinking that would bring them around. Nope. They kept sleeping. And from that point on, they were known among faculty and staff as being the lazy ones, the students who didn't care.

I had a student once tell another group of students that he was leaving orientation because it was, "...a waste of my time..." That didn't go over very well with the Dean of the school, who called him in and requested that he explain just why it was a waste of his time.

- **Soak it In**—There will be serious moments, silly moments, enthralling moments, and boring moments of the orientation process. I encourage you to take it all in and try and learn as much as possible during that time. If you master as much as you can now, you won't have to go back and revisit some of the details that were shared during orientation later in the first or second semester.

- **Enjoy**—Have fun with this. It is a chance to meet your classmates and meet faculty and staff in an environment that is slightly less intense than life will become on a daily basis. Use it as an opportunity to share the wonderful, unique, and talented you to your class and your new university!

For the sake of this book, I am limiting the orientation portion of what to expect to a single chapter and the metaphorical first day. You can expect that orientation will last between 3 and 10 days and will be full of important information that you will at some point need to be successful and to make the most of the coming four years. You can also expect to hear about the curriculum in more detail, a detailed overview of your weekly class schedule, a review of the order of courses you will take in the forthcoming fall and spring semesters, and training on professionalism. You will meet a lot of the faculty and staff, including your academic advisor during this time. You will also take care of nuts-and-bolts-type tasks like getting your student ID, any technology the university provides, as well as hearing about campus safety and security. Welcome to your new home away from home…medical school.

CHAPTER 6

Navigating a Year of Firsts

First, before one begins to actually study for your med school classes, there are some basic study skills that you need to incorporate into your study regime. Second, it's important that you understand that med school is a practice in constructive confusion. Third, practicing general wellness each and every day will be what gets you through this experience.

A Year of Firsts

You have survived the initial day of your new career. Congratulations. Now on to the rest of it. This will be a year of firsts for you: that can be both daunting and exciting. The thought of experiencing new things for the first time can be an invigorating reality that pushes you to embrace new truths and imagine fresh horizons. There are many seasons that encompass life and you have just entered a new dimension. Being a medical student is a daunting task that challenges you in new ways. But those unique challenges can be both brilliantly unexpected and gratifying.

You are going to walk through this new season of life encountering a slew of firsts: your first exam; your first patient encounter; your first disappointing grade; your first positive grade; your first patient birth; and, yes, your first patient death.

Each first will be saved in your memory forever, as these are part of a new season of life that you cannot forget. And that is what is so exciting about this experience. You are not at the beginning of the end, as Winston Churchill once wrote, but rather at the end of the beginning.

In order to outline for you this year of firsts, it's important to understand the big concepts of what you will be faced with during your initial year in med school. The following are the important firsts you will be faced with tackling:

- Developing a new set of study skills that can sustain your success for the remainder of life (far beyond med school you will embark upon a continuing journey of learning).
- Grappling with constructive confusion for the first time.
- Discovering your own brand of personal wellness.
- Avoiding the big trap of anxiety, depression, and despair.
- Managing self-expectations in a year of firsts.

Creating Basic Study Skills
Which Lead to Academic Success

I am frequently asked, a lot, by students (and parents), "What should I do to make sure I am academically successful?"

My response is to list off the **Ten Skills that Lead to Academic Success in Medical School**:

1) **Attend All of Orientation**—Research has clearly shown that students who attend all orientation activities are more academically successful. It's that simple. Whether you think the activities are "boring" or "uncool", attendance makes a difference. I encourage you to attend everything.

2) **Get Organized**—One of the most repeated pieces of advice from the perspective of medical students is to become ultra-organized about how you study, how you plan each week and the time you devote to learning.

   They suggest buying an organizer (digital or paper) with a calendar. Sit down at the end of orientation and review each syllabus and enter the key dates of when exams and practicals are into the calendar. You should then shape your study schedule around when quizzes, exams, and practicals are scheduled. The key phrase should be *no surprises*. It sounds simple…it isn't because you have so much material to track… because it works.

   You then have to be organized on a micro-scale with your day-to-day study schedule. This schedule should be fairly uniform but will change slightly as you get closer to exam dates.

3) **Go to Class**—I don't know how many times I have had to say this to students; from the best students to those who struggle, getting them to go to class is sometimes like pulling teeth. Research from both undergraduate and graduate level institutions shows clearly that students who go to class perform better academically. If you are not doing well and you come to me and say, "...class is such a waste of time...", my initial thought is that you don't know what you are talking about and need to be reminded that attendance equals better performance.

4) **Utilize Resources**—You are paying a lot of money for you to be here. Part of your tuition and fees supports having a variety of resources available to you. I reviewed what those are in the previous chapter. Emphasize using these resources. Tutoring? Yes, please. Counseling services? Yes, please. Student activities? Yes, please.

5) **Professors**—This sounds old school and a bit manipulative, but cozying up to your professors may be a good thing. Investing the time to getting to know your professors is important for your success. I encourage you to get to know your teachers. Always err on the side of going to talk to the professor if you don't understand something in the course. The professor is more likely to give you the benefit of the doubt

if they know you. The sooner the better, in terms of reaching out to the professor, is more effective than becoming hopelessly behind on the course material.

6) **Academic Advisor**—Your academic advisor has an important role in your career in med school. He/she will help advise you on a variety of issues. Talk with them more than the required two or three meetings per academic year. Again, building a relationship with your advisor may pay dividends.

7) **Study Space**—Within the first three weeks of the semester, find a spot, on-campus, in which you like to study. It should be distraction-free and be comfortable. This can be your go-to spot to perform serious study time. Only you know what type of space works for you. Some students enjoy open spaces where people are around, and they wear sound deadening earphones. Some need total privacy and choose a private study room. Find what works for you.

8) **Read**—You are going to have to read in order to survive. Get used to that reality. Whether you are reading from an actual book or from a digital reader, such as an iPad, you will have to read. That is time intensive for most students. If this is something you struggle with, go to a learning specialist at your university and ask for help as soon as you arrive. They can

help you identify high yield information and how to glean that information from the texts you are reading.

9) **Learn How to Answer Second and Third-Order Questions**—You need to learn how to master multiple choice questions well. Why? Because these are the types of questions you will have on your licensing exams. If you come from a college/university which did not provide multiple choice exams, you have some self-reprogramming to do.

Go meet with a learning specialist and have them walk you through how to tackle second and third-order questions which give you a description of a patient and then expect for you to answer several queries from that case study. They can help you identify what is being asked, what is in the case study as a distractor, and how to answer the question properly. Practice, practice, practice these types of questions.

10) **Don't Worry About Career...Yet**—Do not ask anything about board preparation or the residency match during your first semester. First and foremost, you don't need to work on either during your first year. So just simply don't worry about them.

There is plenty of time to figure out what you are going to do with the rest of your life. Your emphasis should be focused upon learning how to be a medical student first, then you can add more responsibility onto your plate once you get to year two. Faculty members will become irritated with you if you continue to ask questions about preparing for boards and the residency match. My advice would be to hold off on that consideration during the first year.

Developing a New Set of Study Skills

Your learning specialists are the real experts, on-campus, as to how to hone your study skills for your benefit. The truth is that you will bring both good and bad study skills with you from your undergraduate years. There may be some skills and habits you developed in the past that are not helpful and will only cause you problems.

For example, memorization only works when there is a finite amount of material for you to review and memorize. In my experience, the volume of material you have to consume and understand is beyond what the normal human brain can stuff into short term memory for a test. So pure memorization doesn't work well. Don't employ that as a technique for learning.

There are also some skills and habits that you formed during undergrad that are positive and will continue to work for you. However, don't expect that you will have to erase all former study skills and habits and build an entirely new set of skills.

How do you figure out what works and what doesn't work? First, I would suggest that you make an appointment with your learning specialist to go over the study plan that you develop for your weekly study schedule. Second, as part of that conversation, talk with them about how you plan to study during the six hours per day of uninterrupted quality study time that you will have to dedicate to post classroom learning (remember...we calculated it out). What specific steps will you take to study? This helps the learning specialist get an idea of your method. Then he/she can advise you on how to go from there, what to eliminate from your method, and what specific techniques to add into your method.

There are certainly a lot of different ways to skin this cat. But in my experience, there are a few solid, time proven study techniques that are most commonly endorsed by medical students:

Recorded Lectures—The most common study method that med students use is to review video-recorded lectures, made available by most medical schools for review of material. Each school will have a technology platform that allows you to download the lecture and review it at normal speed or at varying faster speeds. Most students tell me that they review material at a fast speed of 1.25 or 1.50 faster than normal speed. This makes your professor's voice sound a bit like the Chipmunks but allows you to review the lecture faster.

By reviewing the lecture again, it does a couple of things for you: 1) It is a review of previously covered material, which you will find out is critically important for retention of the material, and, 2) it ensures that you don't miss any important high yield information that was shared by the professor which might end up on the exam.

Reviewing Course Material—Reviewing material multiple times is the key to the kingdom in terms of learning and retaining the information. Learning specialists encourage students to review your course material a minimum of *FIVE* times before you are tested on that material, as that gives your brain multiple opportunities to synthesize and retain what you are studying.

How does one ensure you find time for five full reviews of the material? Well, remember organization and the six hours per day you have to study. I would suggest you break your six hours of daily study time into chunks of time to review new material that was taught that day and, only then, time to review material that was taught on previous days. For example, if you spend two-thirds of your study time reviewing the day's lectures and reading the text that is assigned, then one-third of your study time should be spent reviewing previously lectures and course material that was taught earlier in the course.

Your goal should be that you fully review all course material for a particular exam five times before you take that exam. Reviewing that material can take on many shapes and students use a variety of techniques in order to review old and new material:

- **Flash Cards**—The good old flash card. Many students use these. They make them themselves. There are also online apps that provide pre-made flash cards for medical students on particular course content (you obviously would have to purchase these on your own).

- **Re-Writing Lecture Notes**—Some students take notes, in class during a lecture, and then go home that night and re-write and re-organize their notes, as a review technique. I will warn you that if you aren't a fast writer, this can be a time-consuming way to spend study time.

- **Mnemonics**—The use of mnemonic devices to help you remember old and new material is helpful to many students. Mnemonics are any kind of memory related device/learning technique that aids you in retrieving that information from your memory. In fact, some professors will actually teach material and provide mnemonic devices as part of their lectures to help students retain the information the professor believes is high yield.

- **Drawing**—This technique is used most widely for your anatomy courses. Drawing out the structure that is being taught not only helps one to begin to retain the information about the structure but add a visual learning element to ensure you can identify said structure.

- **Question Banks (Q-Banks)**—Technology has revolutionized the way question banks are used by medical students, as they have been placed in the cloud where they are easily accessible for use and can be reviewed on a variety of devices.

  These Q-banks can be purchased by subject matter to match course material you are currently studying. There are also free Q-banks available online, although

I would caution you to make sure you review their quality as the free Q-banks may not be as high quality and challenging as those you purchase.

- **Other Online Tools**—There are a variety of new and innovative study aids available online for students. It is big business. From Q-banks, to flash cards, to drawing apps, to platforms that link students' work together, there are a plethora of options.

  I am hesitant to endorse specific products, as I don't use them enough these days to know their efficacy. That said, I would encourage you to talk to your learning specialist about what they hear is working well. Talk to your classmates as well. They will offer you unvarnished reviews of anything they have purchased.

Grappling with Constructive Confusion in Medical School

The most significant academic reality that students will face is the concept of *Constructive Confusion*. The concept of constructive confusion is the result of a curriculum filled with courses that don't always provide easily understood concepts, while students are being pushed to think about these ideas in ways that can be new and, on occasion, frustrating. Add the intense load of 5 or 6 science courses on top of that base level of confusion and it can soon become overwhelming to any med student.

STRAIGHT TALK FOR MEDICAL STUDENTS

Students may find themselves in the first course where there can be varying diagnoses of a particular issue that a patient may be reporting. As in life, not everything is black and white. You may have to explain a bioethical issue that has two defendable positions and a continuum of possible issues in between those polar positions. Again, not everything is obvious. They may find themselves in one course talking about how a system within the human body may overlap and connect with another system in confusing ways. Again, not everything is cut and dry, which causes frustration within medical students who are looking for a single correct answer, for ways to understand concepts in easily digestible factoids.

The bottom line is you will read about things you have never before considered; you will have to talk about things in class which you have never discussed. And from a clinical perspective, the same amorphous issue may be true; you will see and experience things with patients that will be confusing, frustrating and, sometimes, completely new to you.

This is what constructive confusion is about. I have had many students say things like, "…this course is so hard…", "I read the material but don't completely understand it…", and, "I feel stupid and unprepared even though I am doing the reading…"

Constructive confusion is what happens when you begin to think critically for yourself. And it is a good thing. But it can also be a frustrating process of reprogramming the mind. As your brain changes, becoming more comfortable and deals with more abstract concepts, differential diagnoses, and third-order questions, so will your success grow. When I talk with students about critically thinking and the confusion that comes with that acquired skill, I encourage you to consider 5 things that you need to keep in mind as you encounter this confusion:

1) **Retrain the Brain**—You are retraining your brain to study differently than you did in undergrad. It takes time and a bit of discomfort to begin to think on a higher plane. Hang in there.

2) **It's OK to Not Know**—It is ok if you don't understand. Own it and don't be afraid to go to the professor for help. We aren't training know-it-alls; we are training humble physicians who know when to ask for help.

3) **The World is Gray**—Not everything is black and white. Sometimes you are studying material that isn't obvious in its clarity. Don't let the gray of the world and one's course material scare you away from becoming a better medical student.

4) **Foolish Equals Not Asking**—There is no stupid question...only stupidity in not asking the question. It's ok to wait until after class to query the professor: wait until the class has cleared out and then go speak with your teacher, if you are nervous to ask him/her the question in the presence of others.

5) **Overwhelmed is a Normal Feeling**—Get comfortable with feeling overwhelmed by some subject matter. It is just the beginning of not understanding everything you will be confronted with in life. Welcome to the club.

Discovering Your Brand of Personal Wellness

A significant challenge of med school you will encounter, that I really wish to stress with you, relates to your personal well-being. For the first time in your life, you will be fully in charge of your own personal success in a demanding, ultra-stressful world of med school. If your gut reaction to that statement is to react negatively and in a concerned way about your ability to live successfully, then you need to pay extra close attention to what I want to share.

First, I have to admit to you that as someone who sits inside medical education and observes students on a daily basis, this is the thing that new medical students struggle with the most, all the while believing you know exactly how to do it. You tend to be overly confident in this category of firsts. Young adults, because you are relatively inexperienced at life, don't perceive what you don't know, and this idea applies quickly and directly to the concept of self-care. I have seen students try and exist on 4 hours of sleep per night. I have seen medical students gain almost 100 pounds in one year, and on the flip side, those who lose 100 pounds in a year to the point where they have been hospitalized.

One has to feel for any student in this kind of situation, as they are trying to learn to care for themselves at a time when they are also trying to move toward the rest of life and handle the stresses of the curriculum simultaneously. It certainly isn't easy and just like so many of the rest of us, this is one place where our humanity, our personhood, is revealed.

The university, if it is worth its salt, will try and help define for you just what general wellness and self-care means. They will provide a wide-ranging definition that should point you in a direction. The school might even have a student-run wellness committee that advocates for students' physical care issues and then communicates with students about how wellness and self-care should play a role in their day-to-day lives. That is all to the good. But it does not replace your role as the person who has to create and implement a wellness plan in your own life. So, I am reminding you, in a non-threatening, non-demeaning way, that self-care matters if you want to be successful later in your life as a physician and there are several key elements to wellness:

Financial Wellness—Not many people would argue that medical students are aware of being financially well or not; I agree. Most med students struggle to make ends meet financially and most of them have considered the debt levels that they are assuming in order to pay for their education. One can understand why this is the case. But reinforcing the importance of managing your monthly budget, so that you don't run into financial problems, is extremely important. In addition, helping you to monitor your individual debt loads and any loans you may have taken on is important to your long-term financial health and wellness.

Intellectual Wellness—One of the great outcomes of attending med school is being immersed within a community that values scholastic, co-curricular, cultural, and community-based activities. All of these activities feed the life of the mind and lead to intellectual wellness. An active mind is a healthy mind.

And being surrounded by super-smart people doesn't hurt. I have attended many activities on-campus that I would venture to guess have enhanced not only the social needs of students but also the life of the mind. Nobel laureates, gifted physicians, experts on LGBTQAI healthcare, and bioethicists all have visited campus recently. These types of opportunities are what I am talking about when I talk about intellectual wellness.

If your school is doing its job right, it will contribute to your intellectual wellness by promoting the following:

1) Improving students' study and learning skills with the goal being to create critically thinking physicians.
2) Promotion of community service through medical workshops or health screenings within their local communities.
3) Participating in international medical mission work.
4) Exposing students to top speakers and presenters in the scientific and medical worlds.

5) Encouraging students to first, identify, and then communicate their thoughts and perceptions in order to enhance their communication skills.

6) Encouraging students to learn how to speak publicly.

Physical and Emotional Wellness—Remaining physically and emotionally well are key to overall success and beyond. Each person in this world defines being healthy in different ways. For one person, it could be having a body fat percentage of less than 10%. For another, it could be maintaining their sobriety. For yet another, it could be walking three miles a day. It varies greatly depending upon the person and their own personal goals and aspirations in terms of maintaining their own wellness.

What we know in higher education is that decades of research clearly indicate that students who are physically and emotionally healthy are more successful academically. It therefore is critical that you be prepared to invest in your own overall wellness. What do I mean by physical and emotional wellness?

As a future physician it is very important that you practice personal wellness on a daily, weekly, and monthly basis. And when we talk with students about what is encompassed in the term general wellness, we are talking about the inclusion of the following:

- **Sleep Health**—Sleep is so important. If I were to say the top three issues students struggle with during med school, lack of good sleep would be one of them. If you are a student who knows that you operate best on nine hours each night, then you need to preserve that nine hours of sleep in order to maintain your overall degree of wellness. Don't sacrifice sleep for study time. What we know is that students who maintain good, healthy sleep habits are more successful academically.

- **Regular Exercise**—Researchers have known for decades that regular exercise has many health benefits. For students who are dealing with complicated academic material on a daily basis, exercise is key to success. The great thing about exercise is that there are multiple options, so do what you are comfortable with. You don't have to run a marathon a day in order to maintain good exercise habits. Walking, lifting weights, yoga, dancing, jogging, rowing, etc. are all great options. Most schools will have student organizations that organize daily or weekly workouts for their members. Keep an eye out for exercise opportunities on-campus.

- **Mental Health**—So much of what we are talking about in this section is interconnected, as healthy sleep, regular exercise, good diet, and holistic spiritual health all contribute to one's mental health and wellness. I encourage students to think about the fact that one's wellness is linked to overall mental health.

  If you are someone who has employed a therapist in the past to maintain your overall wellness, continue using that resource. The vast majority of med schools provide free counseling for students. If you are someone who takes medication, to maintain your wellness, don't stop taking your medication.

- **Healthy Diet**—One of the most common mistakes med students make is not eating well or consistently. They skip meals. They eat out of vending machines. It's a recipe for disaster.

  Making sure you are eating well during your med school years is so important. This is possible even when you are not the next Barefoot Contessa. Make sure you give yourself time in your schedule for eating meals each day.

Spiritual Wellness—Medical students develop in a variety of ways during their training years. They develop intellectually, socially, and spiritually. For most students, their spiritual development is tied directly to the religion they practiced when they were living at home. Other students may grow to not perceive themselves as religious but do see themselves as having some kind of spiritual foundation.

For medical students who are training in an environment that is so closely connected to life and death, the proximity to life's uncertainties does have an impact on them, personally and spiritually. I have physician friends who see death on a daily basis, who don't think twice about the finality of life and rarely think of it from a spiritual perspective. For other physicians, their religious beliefs are incredibly important to them in the context of what they do for a living.

Either way, you will continue to develop a belief system informed by your family beliefs and your training as a physician. Understanding that this will happen, helps you to cultivate your own belief structure. Some of it may remain the same, some parts may change, or your belief structure may shift significantly. Be aware that all college and universities have ties to local churches, mosques, and synagogues, and can help you to find a church home should you desire that religious connection.

Social Wellness—Students should be happy and by our nature, human beings search for friendship, community, and an affinity group with which to be connected. This is why social wellness is so important during these years. Med students have a finite amount of time to socialize because of their schedules and the demands of school.

That said, just because your schedule is limited does not mean you should skip socially connecting with your classmates, other students, and adults in the surrounding communities. Being grounded socially remains especially important. Do not skip out on social opportunities as you will be losing out on the important social connections that we all crave. You will miss the enriching opportunities that interacting with other human beings provides. But just do it smartly and with good solid boundaries to limit the amount of time you spend participating. Find a solid group of friends, which may change over time, and be honest with yourself if it is not working out the way you thought. There are plenty of students who are welcoming of your joining their friend group.

Health and Wellness Mistakes—Over 25 years, I have seen students make a lot of mistakes in terms of stewarding their own health and wellness. Common health and wellness mistakes made by medical students include:

- Taking unprescribed medication provided by a friend.
- Adopting unhealthy, self-destructive habits involving alcohol and drug use.
- Going off one's prescribed medication without physician approval.
- Exacerbating eating disorders through poor diet management.
- Failing to develop a primary care physician relationship while in school.

Don't fall into these traps. Not only can they cause you personal problems, they can end your career in a variety of ways. If you don't want to practice wellness for yourself, do it for your professional life. It will ensure you stay on track to becoming a physician.

In summary, if you are able to cultivate your personal wellness in the ways I have outlined above, you will be better off having tried to accomplish some or all of those factors that make up personal wellness; which, after all, is just an academic's term for a healthy, happy, well-adjusted you.

Avoiding the Dangerous Trap of Anxiety, Depression, and Despair

There is a growing trend in higher education that is rapidly reaching epidemic proportions as it relates to the mental health condition of students, the amount of mental health services colleges/universities may provide, and the number of mental health emergencies occurring on campuses nation-wide.

Based upon my own experience, over the last ten years I saw a marked increase in the number of students needing and utilizing mental health services that we provide. Not only were usage numbers up, but the number of students coming to us already having had therapy or being diagnosed with a mental health condition increased markedly on an annual basis, as well. The number of students coming to college already on some type of psychotropic medication has exploded in the last decade, and we saw incremental increases year-over-year of students already on medication.

There are some positive outcomes related to this reality. First, we as a society are finally talking about and treating mental health issues in a more transparent, proactive, and consistent manner. In addition, we are treating mental health issues like other illness, which is the way we should be treating them. If one has the flu or an upper-respiratory infection, one goes to a physician to be treated. Similarly, we have become more comfortable with treating depression and anxiety like other illnesses. This is a positive development as twenty years ago, mental health issues among college students were ineffectively swept under the rug by some institutions, parents, and even the students themselves. That was not good for overall student wellness.

There remain concerns about your generation of students, however. Research clearly indicates that your generation is more depressed and anxious than previous groups. What are the facts about mental health and this current generation of college/medical students? They are the following:

- More anxious and depressed than prior generations.
- Suicidality is also higher among this generation.
- More medicated for mental health issues than previous generations.
- Seeking more treatment from mental health professionals than earlier generations.

In a recent study, conducted on 10,000 medical students currently enrolled at osteopathic medical schools (study conducted by the Council for Osteopathic Student Government Presidents—COSGP), it was discovered that 54% of the 10,000 medical students claimed to be clinically depressed and/or anxious at one point or another during their four years of medical school. Fifty-four percent! If 54% of a college campus had meningitis or even the flu, we would close that campus and declare an epidemic. Yet, educators still struggle to effectively cope with the influx of the number of students with mental health issues. This is neither for lack of trying nor for lack of resources. Most colleges and universities are actively investing more and more funding in the areas of counseling services as well as overall health services, too.

Why, then? Why is this generation struggling with mental health issues at greater rates than earlier generations? The answers are not clear, but I want to try and illuminate what we do know for you, because we know that this experience can elevate levels of depression.

Anxiety—If I had a dollar for every medical student who came through my office door, in the last ten years, to tell me that they are feeling anxious, I would be a very rich man. Universities are seeing a rush of students who are sharing that they are terrified to take exams, nervous about their success and goals, apprehensive to seek treatment, apprehensive to tell their parents, and generally worried about their lives.

The fact is that a very large percentage of medical students are experiencing regular or continuing bouts of anxiety. A recent research study published in the International Journal of Environmental Research and Public Health indicates that 34% of medical students experience anxiety on a regular basis. This is substantially higher than the general population at 18%.

What does this mean for you? I would encourage you to think about how you are feeling in your own life. Do you demonstrate traits of anxiousness? Do you know what the common variables of anxiety are in the general population? Read up on this and make sure you are self-monitoring to ensure that if you do exhibit signs of anxiety, you reach out for help.

If you have experienced episodes of unease already in your life, what are you doing to proactively deal with your anxiety? Meeting with a counselor to learn ways to reduce anxiousness is a first step. Sitting down with your physician to talk about medication options is also another step you can take. Learning and practicing mindfulness and meditation is another proactive step you can take to reduce the impact of anxiety.

The bottom line for this year of firsts is: if you have already experienced anxiety, be prepared for increased levels in medical school and a need to continue to be proactive. If you are new to feelings of anxiety, ask for help.

Depression—Similarly, if I had a dollar for all the medical students who have come to my office demonstrating the core components of clinical depression, I would again be very wealthy.

Anxiety and depression sometimes go together, which means I hear a lot of students sharing a list of symptoms that are appropriate in diagnosing both conditions. So, what should you watch for as a medical student? The following changes in behaviors which may be an indication that you or a friend are experiencing depression:

- Increase in academic problems.
- Depressive symptoms, such as a down mood, sadness, or loss of interest.
- Sharp mood swings.
- Withdrawal from friends, family, and classmates.

- Feelings of hopelessness.
- Drastic changes in personal appearance.
- Increases in substance abuse.

What behaviors can you promote within yourself to help you combat the potential onslaught of depressive symptoms? Encourage yourself to do the following:

- Eat well. You need to eat on a regular schedule and eat healthy foods. I have seen far too many medical students feeding themselves out of vending machines on a regular basis. This is not a recipe for either effective nutrition or for overall wellness.
- Sleep well. You should go to sleep generally at the same time each night and get up at the same time each morning. Build sleep into your daily schedule.
- Avoid caffeine. Or in a first effort to cut back on caffeine, don't have any after 6 p.m. Please, please, please avoid energy drinks which have dubious ingredients.
- Avoid use of alcohol and other substances.
- Limit, or eliminate, use of social media. There are many studies that demonstrate that frequent usage of social media can heighten levels of both depression and feelings of hopelessness.
- Avoid isolation. We are social beings who need to interact with others. Depressed people should not be alone. If you find yourself sitting in your apartment for the thirteenth day in a row, without having talked to a

friend, seen a classmate, or talked to your family, this is a danger sign.

- Encourage yourself to talk to a counselor. The vast majority of campuses have free counseling options available for students.

- Go to talk to a physician or encourage the friend you are concerned about to see a doctor.

- University staff, who are all well-trained on how to deal with these issues, are waiting to assist you or someone you are worried about.

Lacking Resilience—Medical schools, colleges, and universities are seeing yet another nation-wide, troubling trend: a near doubling of emergency calls to their counseling services offices. However, when the staff analyze the reasons behind why a student is reaching out, defining the issue as an "emergency", they are surprised by some of the reasons why students perceive that they are in need of emergent help.

One college administrator shared a story of a freshman student who was so upset by being called a 'bitch' by her roommate that she called the University's emergency line seeking counseling help immediately. Another campus dealt with students calling the emergency hotline because they returned to campus on a weekend and were not able to find a parking space within reasonable walking distance from their residence hall.

I can share many similar stories...the mother of a student calling me to ask me if I or my staff could awaken him each morning each morning for class because he was struggling to get out of bed. I politely declined and reminded her that he was training to be a physician. How could we trust him to save lives if he cannot be trusted to get out of bed on his own each morning?

Dr. Jean Twenge and Dr. Angela Duckworth have noted that this generation of students clearly lacks resilience and that we as a society need to provide our young adults with the opportunities and skills necessary to build what may also be termed "grit".

Dr. Duckworth has written a NY Times Best Seller entitled "*Grit*" that is the best book I have read on this subject. In her book, she highlights that grit is defined as perseverance and that perseverance and passion drive the effort and commitment to meet the goals, we set for ourselves. It is not a terribly complex concept. But what we are seeing today is more and more medical students arriving on-campus lacking that essential determination to push forward when one meets obstacles. For too long, she hypothesizes, students' parents have served to push those obstacles out of the way. As a result, the student has not developed the skills appropriate to perseverance. So how do parents and college educators help students to build grit and resilience?

Dr. Duckworth emphasizes two important factors to keep in mind: First, effort is everything. Even though society has said that hard work trumps pure talent, we may not actually believe ourselves when we parrot that or other aphorisms. But we should. Hard work, the effort we put into studying, athletics, clubs, organizations, friendships, relationships and everything else we do daily has a bigger impact on success than just having the talent to perform a task acceptably. Duckworth's research shows us that the effort we put into a goal is twice as impactful than talent alone. Second, small goals matter. If we approach each day by setting small goals towards our larger objectives, we can overcome the daily obstacles that often stand in the way of our success. Small wins lead to daily success and keep us motivated to continue to succeed.

The American Psychological Association is so concerned about this lack of "grit" in Americans, in general, that they have a section of their website dedicated to "*The Road to Resilience*" and recommend Nine Ways to Build Resilience:

1) **Make Connections**—Connections with family, friends, and colleagues are all positive. Avoid locking yourself away.

2) **Avoid Viewing Crises as Insurmountable**—Crises come with life. Life's twists and turns happen whether we want them to happen or not. You cannot avoid bad things happening or problems arising. Changing your world view to understand that unpleasant issues happen will help you feel as if they aren't so overwhelming.

3) **Change is Part of Life**—Just as life has crises, so life also presents us with the need for change. There are many people who don't deal well with having to adopt to doing things differently. Working to become more open to change can lead to less anxiety when it is forced upon you.

4) **Move Toward Goals**—Encouraging yourself to always be moving toward your goals, even when it feels like you are only taking baby steps is an important concept. As long as positive progress is being made, you can remain hopeful you are heading in a positive direction.

5) **Be Decisive**—Decisiveness rather than detachment is key. Rather than shutting down and avoiding making a decision, encourage yourself to be decisive about even one small thing so that you remain focused on the issue.

6) **Self-Discovery is Good**—People who have dealt with adversity and made it to the other side report feeling as if they have better relationships, an increased sense of self-worth, and a greater perception of personal strength. When something bad happens, encourage yourself to look inward as to what you can learn from the pain and hardship involved.

7) **Nurture a Positive View of Oneself**—It is so important that medical students begin to trust themselves and their own instincts. Self-trust helps to build resilience.

8) **Maintain Hope**—Optimism works. Visualize the result or outcome you want rather than worrying about the potential negative outcomes. (Visualize yourself in a hospital setting, sitting with a patient, talking and solving, as best possible, that patient's problem(s).)

Beginning to visualize success can result in feelings of hope and enhanced self-worth.

9) **Self-Care is Critical**—Always encourage yourself to take care of yourself first. If you focus on self-care, you will have the strength to deal with the moments that are challenging and, in turn, be able to offer care to others.

I cannot stress how important resilience is to success in college, graduate school, medical school, law school, married life, parenthood, and most other parts of life. If you can practice the key traits to resilience, or grit, on a regular basis, you will reinforce for yourself the resilience skills you need to continually develop.

Medicated Generation—Research clearly indicates that your generation of students have grown up in a society which chooses to medicate students who are struggling with depression, anxiety, and other psychosocial issues. The number of students in this generation who arrive already on psychotropic medication is at an all-time high.

I have worked with students who wanted to take psychotropic medication, as well as those who were adamantly opposed to such treatment. There are very real and legitimate arguments both in favor and against taking such medication. Here's what I have observed over a 25-year career: in situations where a student is really struggling and one's academic progress is being impacted by the depression or anxiety that they are experiencing, medication, along with meeting regularly with a counselor is a treatment plan that has proven to offer excellent outcomes. Many students have said (I am paraphrasing numerous conversations), "The medication has helped so much...it takes the edge off the depression that I was feeling... and it helps me to focus better than I was able to before the medication..."

For students who have more difficult and complex diagnoses, the use of medication to control personality or psychotic disorders become a veritable requirement for success. I have encountered many students in this, or a similar kind of situation and such a diagnosis can make graduating from medical school difficult...but not impossible.

I had a fourth-year, 26 year old, medical student, who experienced a psychotic break while on a surgery rotation. The hospital at which he was rotating notified us immediately. He was taken off rotation immediately and we worked with the state's local Physician's Health Program to have him assessed, hospitalized, and treated. He was diagnosed as bi-polar. We then put the student on a medical leave of absence for more than a year while he underwent in-patient, and eventually out-patient treatment. He returned 18 months later and completed the remaining requirements for his medical degree and is now a third-year resident successfully navigating work, personal life, and maintaining his health. Medication and regular therapy with a counselor were a must for him and he continues to have both as a continued part of his on-going treatment plan. Medication and therapy are a must for any student navigating such conditions.

One bit of advice I will reiterate more than once in this book is that if you are already on psychotropic medication when you arrive, *you should not go off that medication* unless approved by your physician. I have seen, more times than I can count, students arrive thinking it is a "new phase in life..." and then make the decision to stop taking their medication, without consulting their physician. This decision invariably ends badly for the student. Because medical school is a transition and transitions all too frequently causes us stress, I do not recommend going off any medication designed to minimize stress and its by-products (i.e. anxiety and/or depression).

There are both clear upsides and downsides to going on medication. Understanding the pros and cons of this decision is the responsible way of reaching an appropriate and thoughtful conclusion. On the upside of the decision, medical school staffs are becoming more comfortable with addressing and treating mental illness like any other disease or condition. And we are talking about such issues more openly and honestly with students than ever before. If you begin to struggle, it should be comforting to know that there are multi-faceted layers of support designed by administrators and faculty to identify the problem and provide the necessary help. But, if you identify that you are struggling, before someone at the university identifies that a problem exists, call the Office of Student Services to give them a heads-up and ask for help.

From the downside perspective, we have a pretty clear picture as to why students may grow depressed and anxious in the pressure-cooker environment. Unfortunately, identification of the variables we have discussed here too often represents things that have already occurred. That said, there are steps you can take during your med school experience to make sure you are both taken care of and supported. It's also an opportunity for you (and your family) to identify and alter decisions and behaviors that may have contributed to your current situation. The downside is that this is a bummer, but it can be fixed. That is a positive message at the end of a difficult section.

In this year of firsts, being on medication is okay. Having to go on medication for the first time is okay too. Both are okay as long as the end result is the you are feeling better and are able to perform academically at a capable level. Remember that the goal is your success.

Suicidal—The American College Health Association (ACHA) indicates that suicide rates among young adults ages 15-24 have TRIPLED since the 1950s. In addition, they have identified that suicide is the second most common cause of death among college students. As if these statistics are not concerning enough, on any given day on a college campus, 6 out of 10 college students may confess having seriously considered attempting suicide in the last 12 months.

In addition to these alarming statistics, medical students and physicians commit suicide at nearly double the national rate. A 2004 study in the Journal of American Psychiatry found that female physicians are at higher risk for attempting suicide than their male counterparts. They are 250% more likely to attempt suicide.

We, medical educators, as well as physicians in training, want to always keep in mind that we have a responsibility to be observant of the warning signs associated with suicidal thoughts and behaviors. The American Foundation for the Prevention of Suicide outlines three categories of suicidal behavior:

What the Medical Student is Saying—Is the student talking about any of the following?

- Killing themselves.
- Feeling hopeless.
- Having no reason to live.
- Being a burden to others.
- Feeling trapped.
- Experiencing unbearable emotional pain.

How the Medical Student is Behaving—Is the student behaving in any of the following ways?

- Increasing their use of drugs and alcohol.
- Looking for a way to end their life, such as searching online for methods.
- Withdrawing from activities.
- Isolating themselves from family and friends.

133

- Sleeping too much or not at all.
- Demonstrating aggression and/or anger.
- Demonstrating fatigue.

The Medical Student's Mood—Is the student displaying one or more of the following moods?
- Depression
- Anxiety
- Loss of interest
- Irritability
- Humiliation/shame
- Agitation or anger
- Relief/sudden improvement

As someone who will be charged with maintaining the health and well-being of others, it is vitally important that you, 1) take your own health and well-being seriously; 2) that you observe the health and well-being of your classmates and notify university administrators if you suspect a fellow student is struggling; and, 3) play a leadership role, on-campus, in ensuring that you and your fellow students are educated of the signs and symptoms of suicide and know how to proactively seek assistance if you, or someone else, is struggling.

In a year of firsts, no one wants to experience the devastating aftermath of suicide. Remember the oath you will take during your White Coating Ceremony about doing no harm. Make sure to do no harm to yourself. Equally as important, make sure your classmates don't harm themselves.

NAVIGATING A YEAR OF FIRSTS

Managing Self-Expectations
in a Year of Firsts

As I have talked with second, third, and fourth year medical students about what advice they have for you, a theme has surfaced that may be important to share. You are in a tough spot because the fanfare of being in medical school comes with a lot of expectations from people in your life: parents, siblings, grandparents, aunts and uncles, friends, former teachers, coaches, etc. Sometimes those expectations are fair and sometimes the expectations are unrealistically heightened and are, therefore, unfair. You will have to manage such expectations on your own. Some will be easy to cast aside, and others will be incredibly hard to ignore.

Similarly, you will have expectations for yourself as you begin this experience. This can be a good thing, as I have earlier discussed with you the importance of creating personal and professional goals for yourself. Goals are certainly expectations. Anytime we create expectations for ourselves, we want them to be realistic, achievable, and something that advances us towards positive achievement.

Many of the medical students I have spoken with, as I started to think about this book, said that some of the expectations they had for themselves were either not realistic, naïve, or surprisingly unexpected. In other words, they created an expectation that they, in retrospect, didn't realize was there until they did not, or could not, meet their own self-imposed expectations.

There were three examples that came up pretty consistently within students' first-year where self-expectation simply did not match reality:

First Standardized Patient Encounter—I think students visualize what their first standardized patient encounter will be like. They picture themselves walking into the room and being a dynamic, reassuring physician and that they will both charm their patients and help them to feel at ease. But rarely does it work that way, at least in the beginning.

For introverted students the encounter is much harder than they expected. "I walked into the room and just froze. I didn't know what to say and how to say it. I felt embarrassed and paralyzed…"

For extroverted students, the encounter was also much more difficult than they expected. "I walked into the room and had a big smile on my face and was really outgoing. After the experience was over, the patient shared that she was put off by my overly happy attitude…it didn't work."

Learning to walk the fine line between welcoming/ professional and coming off as brash/arrogant is a challenge for students. Similarly, the line between being perceived as welcoming/warm or cold/non-empathic is also challenging to determine without practice. What students thought would be their strength before having their first patient encounter was actually what tripped them up in the end.

The good news is that you have many chances to develop an acceptable approach before you become involved in clinical rotations working with real patients. And that practice is what helps you to hone your skills and use your personal gifts that you bring to the table, as a future physician, to a mutually beneficial advantage when meeting with a patient.

First Anatomy Lab—"I walked into the lab for our first experience with the cadaver and there was this body on our table in front of us…it looked nothing like I expected it to look. It was cold and inhuman in many ways. And we were expected to begin dissecting it…cutting it open. I felt sick and started to cry. My brother had died 6 months earlier, and I didn't think that would come rushing back to me, but it did, and I didn't know how to cope with that…"

This student's personal loss triggered her when she stepped into the anatomy lab for the first time and started thinking about the dissection that was about to take place. Understandably, she wasn't emotionally ready for this experience.

This student was not the only student who was impacted by the first few weeks of anatomy lab. Many students aren't prepared for what happens in these labs, as it is an assault on the senses: the visuals are difficult, the actual physical action of cutting into a human body can be distressing, to say nothing about the smells not being something one is used to in daily life.

In this specific instance, this student's expectations for how she would respond the first time she was in lab did not match what actually occurred. And that was okay. One of the anatomy professors noticed her color had changed and saw tears forming in her eyes and escorted her out of the lab. The professor also connected her with one of the university's counselors to ensure she had someone to process the death of her brother with and to talk about ways to separate the professional expectations in the lab from the trauma of losing a family member.

First Exposure to Being a Student Doctor—"We stood up on stage, with our White Coats on, and had just taken our oath…and I thought to myself, I don't like being called student doctor. I don't like the responsibility that comes with that label. Especially considering I haven't even completed my first day in med school. I have no idea what I am doing!"

For some, being called Student Doctor is a great motivator and something to strive towards as they progress. For others, the idea of being labeled Student Doctor is a frightening reality once they are called that for the first time, as they don't like being regarded as something that is so far from the truth in terms of knowledge, skills, and abilities.

"I didn't like being called Student Doctor. It scared me. I thought I would like it before I got here, but once you are here you realize how far you have to go before you should be called doctor or physician. I definitely felt the weight and expectations of the title."

Closing Thoughts

There is no doubt that this year of firsts will reveal a whole new world to you as a student, investigator, detective, professional, and human being. You will be challenged to develop a new set of study skills and a study plan that will, hopefully, yield academic success, while you grapple with the frustration of constructive confusion. Your health and well-being will depend upon your discovery and cultivation of your own brand of wellness, while avoiding the traps laid by conditions such as anxiety and depression. And you will be tested in how you manage your own self-expectations for key parts of this educational experience.

Your training will certainly offer moments of clarity, while also proffering ambiguous moments that seem to lead nowhere. It is my belief that your qualifications, skills, knowledge, and passion will be enough to guide you through the murky moments of confusion. Arrive knowing that you won't and can't predict everything you will be exposed to, but know that you are well qualified to handle everything that will be passed your way.

CHAPTER 7

Surviving Year One: All the Advice No One Else Will Give You

O ne of the great advantages of being an insider is that you get to hear all of the feedback provided by current, new, and former students, from parents, from faculty and staff, and alumni. Over my 25-year career, I have received a lot of feedback and suggestions. The best feedback I have received is from students is those morsels of advice they wish they had received, but no one shared with them. They usually share that piece of wisdom and reflect on the fact that if they had been aware of the issue or question, it would have made their time much easier, more enjoyable, and/or more meaningful.

For years, I collected a list of bits of wisdom from all of these constituents and about 5 years ago, I started to share these bits of advice with new students. I would kick all of the faculty and staff out of the room and it went something like this…

Congratulations. You have reached a point in life to which very few people in the world aspire. But this is just the beginning of a new journey, and in order to make it to the end of this challenge, graduation, you will need a certain set of skills to be able to make it through the stress, pressure, challenge, and rigor. What I want to do is provide you with 20 pieces of advice that will be key to both surviving and prospering. These are things you aren't going to hear from other faculty or staff at the University. My hope is that these pieces of advice are honest, direct, unflinching, and helpful.

#1-This Advice Isn't B.S.—Don't dismiss this advice as B.S. because it is yet another in a list of pieces of advice from some old guy. The number one regret that my medical students told me to share with you is (I am paraphrasing their feedback), "I wish I had listened more closely to the advice given at the beginning of my first year of medical school…"

We had a group of first year medical students at a table and asked them for feedback on orientation and there was uniform agreement that they did not listen intently enough to the advice provided from both administrators and their fellow med students. Many of them just didn't listen and take it seriously. It is going to seem a bit intimidating, but remember that in a few short weeks, your classmates will be a group of strong friends to help support you.

#2-Be Competitive Only with Yourself—Some of you may have selected schools which have a culture predicated upon competition. Some of you may have selected schools which are reputedly less competitive. Regardless of the word-of-mouth reputation of your school's culture, I would recommend that the only person you should be competitive with, during your years in med school, is yourself.

About five years ago, a male student in our first-year class was meeting with a professor about an upcoming exam. The professor shared some information with him about what would be covered on the exam. The professor specifically mentioned to him that he had the responsibility of sharing with his classmates what blocks of information would be tested. The student kept the information to himself. He didn't pass it on so that he could have an advantage over his classmates.

Rather than selfishly hold back information that could benefit your entire class, be a good team member and share it when asked to do so. And do not waste your time and energy obsessing about how Jane or Jim Doe did on their Neuroscience exam. Concentrate only on how you did on your neuroscience exam. Set goals for yourself that focus solely on your own abilities and your own performance. Challenge yourself to excel in each course but compete with yourself, alone. Avoid the trap of becoming competitive with your classmates for the following reasons:

1) Being overly competitive creates discord within your class.

2) As a result, classmates begin looking out for themselves first, rather than working as a team.

3) If a "me first" attitude exists within the class, the class loses out on opportunities to help all members become better medical students.

4) "Me first" attitudes reinforce bad behaviors that show up later during the clinical years and residency. You don't want to develop that reputation for yourself.

#3-All Boats Rise with The Tide—*Cooperate and Graduate* should become your class motto. One student's success then becomes another classmate's success. If you approach this with the idea that you can work as a team to ensure that everyone is successful, rather than competing with one another, you will be much happier and more successful.

Learning the value of teamwork is essential to new incoming members of the medical profession. Not only will you need a team to help you get through this successfully, you will need to learn to work in a team, as you will be expected to be a valued medical team member when you venture onward to residency.

This piece of advice connects nicely with the idea of being only competitive with yourself. Selfishness doesn't work well. If you approach your time in med school from the perspective of working in a team, being selfless, and understanding that your success is the success of the group, you will be much better off, to say nothing of happier and with enhanced self-esteem.

"I was really struggling with content in Cardiopulm and had been studying by myself, when a friend convinced me to come to a study group session she and some friends were having. It literally turned my grade around. For the first time, I was understanding the concepts and course material. Hearing someone else explain it to me in a different way than the book and the professor was so helpful..." This comment came from a first year medical student who found that group study was so beneficial to her.

Those students who are doing well and helping other students to understand difficult concepts, participate in tutoring sessions, help study for exams and practicals, and being a good friend to their classmates is what this is about. So be open to a team approach to studying and support. I promise it will help you get through med school more successfully and far happier.

#4-You May Not Know it, But You Have Signed a Social Contract—As soon as you take that oath at your White Coating Ceremony, you now are a working, integral part of the social contract that exists between the medical profession and our society at large. Historically, this social contract has been either unspoken and/or understated. However, once you become a student physician, whether you want to or not, you assume the role of the healer. And in the eyes of society, they assume you are one who possesses and embodies the quietly assured competence, altruistic service, steadfast integrity, accountability, transparency, objective advice, and promotion of the greater good.

Take your social contract seriously, as your medical school will take seriously its social contract to train you well and to ensure that you are a gifted physician who can make a huge difference in our world.

#5-Twenty-Five is the Magic Number—One of the most-asked questions from new medical students is how should they quantify the commitment they need to make in order to be successful? For most, understanding the scope of the commitment they need on a daily, weekly, and monthly basis during med school is something that must be learned and practiced in a disciplined way.

We conducted some internal research and found that students who are able to put in 25 plus hours, per week, of concentrated study outside of class time, have markedly better GPAs in medical school than those who put in 24 hours or less. We were never able to get at the underlying reasons why 25 plus hours was the tipping point for success. That said, the data was compelling.

You need to be prepared to commit 25+ hours, of true concentrated study (not sitting at a desk watching funny YouTube videos all afternoon), apart from class time, each week. What does that entail in a normal 24-hour day and seven-day week?

Let's assume the following time commitments in a 24-hour clock:

Life Essentials
- 8 hours of sleep
- 1 hour for lunch
- 1 hour for dinner
- 1 hour for exercising

Total—11 hours

Academic Essentials
- 4 hours of class
- 3 hours of lab

Total—7 hours

Study Essentials
- 6 hours for study

Total—6 hours

This simple 24-hour clock breaks down how many hours per day for life, academic, and study essentials in an average day. It leaves the student 6 hours, per day, of serious study time. That means 30 hours, Monday through Friday, of study time. Then if you are able to add large 10+-hour blocks on the weekends, you have the opportunity for anywhere between 30 and 50 hours per week.

The bottom-line message of this illustration is that it is absolutely possible to carve out 25 plus hours per week to study outside of class. Program yourself to make the commitment. Part of becoming an organized medical student is mapping out each day to include your life essentials, academic essentials, and study essentials. Employ the huge blocks of available time on the weekends to your advantage, by blocking it out on your daily planner on the weekends for uninterrupted study.

The first response I get from most medical students is, and I am paraphrasing, "I have kids and I want to spend time with them..." or "I need to spend time with my wife..." or "I want to volunteer on the weekends..." There are a laundry list of things that students want or need to do in addition to the hours dedicated above.

I will be the first to tell you that my students advised me to share with you two things on this subject: First, come to your first day of medical school with a study plan sketched out on paper, as you will need to use it right away. Second, build time for yourself into your study schedule. Take breaks, start a new hobby, workout, spend time with your kids; whatever works to give you downtime. There is time to stick to your study plan and time to take for yourself in most weeks of medical school.

Remember that there are 30-50 hours of potential study time per week. If you want to dedicate an extra hour per day to spend time with loved ones, just understand that you have to recoup those hours from somewhere, and study time is where it comes from. So, if you add something to your essentials list, that's fine, but remember to make up for it in another block in your scheduling. This is do-able. This is going to change the way you approach your life (more to come on that). The sooner you can accept that reality, the better off you will be.

#6-There Are No Guarantees in Life—There are no guarantees in medical school, either. No one is saying because you paid tuition that you are guaranteed to be granted your MD or DO degree. Quite the opposite. If you do not pass all of your classes as well as passing all of your licensing exams, you cannot be a physician. Accept that fact of life at the outset.

One of life's great lessons is that there are absolutely no guarantees. I happen to be writing this book during the COVID 19 pandemic. I have been inside my house now for 12 days in a row and I would do just about anything to be able to go outside and interact with other human beings. But alas, I am stuck here for the sake of those I love as well as my own well-being. No one guaranteed that our lives would not be turned upside down during such an unanticipated period of time. We simply have to suck it up and do what we are told to do in order for us to save lives and be healthy and defeat this virus.

This experience will provide challenges, like COVID 19, in that you will be expected to do something that may fall beyond your comfort zone. When confronted with such circumstances you will have to suck it up, pull up your big kid pants, and make it happen, even when you feel as if you cannot.

The moral of this story is getting ready for life to change and change in ways that will make you uncomfortable. One place I have figured out that isn't a comfortable place for whiners is medical school. You will not find many empathetic ears if you want to go into whiney mode. The shortest way out, save for failure, is straight through.

#7-If You Are Sick or in Crisis, Don't Test—Part of the intensity of the experience is that you will have high stakes exams that determine your grade. For example, you may have a course that spans six weeks and during that six-week course, you will have two exams that make up 100% of your course grade. The stakes are high for you to do well on each exam.

I would be a very rich man if I were paid a dollar for each student I have had in my office in tears because they took an exam while they were battling an illness and failed to perform well. Similarly, I have had tearful students in my office who tried to take a high stakes exam when they were enduring a personal emergency. They came to me to request a retake because they were ill. The answer was no.

These exams are too important for you to make a mistake on. Therefore, I always tell them, if you are sick or in crisis, contact the university staff member in charge of coordinating your exams and request a delay (each university will have a specific process for requesting an excused absence, yet another reason for listening closely during orientation). A delay will require that you show a doctor's note excusing you for being sick, but I promise you it will be worth it to wait and take the exam when you aren't facing illness or an emergency.

This is likely the most often ignored piece of advice I give. Therefore, I reinforce it repeatedly. Students get tired of me saying this, but it will impact anywhere between 15-20% of a given class each year.

#8-Own Your Medical School Experience...You Are Paying for This—There is a long-understood fine line for students that exists between the training piece of med school and the fact that they are actual customers who pay a tremendous amount of tuition each year to attend med school.

For many faculty and staff who work at med schools, the fact that you are seeking training in a profession means that you should show up to class and lab and do what you are asked. For many students, the attitude is, and I am once again paraphrasing, "I am paying for this experience: therefore, I should have a say in how the experience proceeds." This tension is real and ever-present.

I encourage all students to realize that their power to make relevant change comes when they speak with one voice as a class. They are the customer and they should be able to make requests within reason, of the administration and faculty and be taken seriously. Unfortunately, that happens less when a single student is advocating for something. But when the entire class speaks with one voice, change can occur. In order to advocate for your class, consider the following:

1) Remember that you are paying for this experience and therefore your medical school needs to listen to its customers.

2) Speak with one voice. Have your class officers communicate directly and regularly with the University administration and faculty.

STRAIGHT TALK FOR MEDICAL STUDENTS

3) When you do advocate for an issue, stick to the facts, be professionally assertive, and speak as an involved group.

#9-Life Isn't Fair...Neither Are Parts of Medical School— Once again, I am going to be honest with you...this is not always a positive experience; nor are parts of it fair. In fact, there are moments that seem either unfair and/or downright wrong. But if it was easy, everyone would be a doctor, right?

There are going to be weeks where you have two or three exams and/or practicals. There are going to be weeks when you feel the weight of the world. There are going to moments when a faculty or administrator says something that upsets you either personally or professionally. Family emergencies are real and do happen while you are training to be a physician. These things are going to happen.

I had a second-year medical student who received that call from family that no one ever wants to receive. Her mother's cancer was terminal, and she only had months to live. She came to my office and we sat down with my team to determine how best to help her handle her situation. We placed her on an emergency leave of absence. She took a semester off and then came back and picked up where she left off. She is now a fourth-year medical student who is about to graduate. And she is grateful to have had personal time with her mom during those final months of her life.

One thing is for certain: medical school will help you develop thicker skin. It will teach you to learn how to suck-it-up and move on. It will challenge you to continually be developing grit and resilience. It will do so because it is not much different than life. There are twists and turns that are reinforced by positive highs and negative lows. Be ready for those, and do not trick yourself into believing that this process will be perfectly positive. It won't be.

#10-Don't Be Stubborn...Ask for Help—Just because you are a medical student doesn't make you immune to academic, personal, or health issues. Unfortunately, life's events don't stop just because you are here. I have seen thousands of students go through this process and one thing that is common among a large percentage of them is that they are stubborn. They have never had to ask for help before, during undergrad, because school and science came easy to them.

Well, I am here to tell you that if you want to navigate this experience successfully, there will be a moment or moments when you need to reach out to someone and ask for help. What kind of help? Ask a classmate for help understanding a class concept. Signing up to have a tutor for a particular class. Seek an appointment with the college psychologist when you are stressed. Go to talk to a professor about course content you don't understand.

The students who are able to set their ego aside and go ask for help will traverse this experience more successfully.

I had a second-year student call my office and request that I meet him in one of our private study rooms. I walked across campus and knocked on the door. He opened the door with tears streaming down his cheeks. Once we both took a chair, I just observed his demeanor. He was crying, breathing heavily, his face was flushed, and his hands were clammy and trembling. He said, "I think I'm having a panic attack…" We began talking about what was wrong and he admitted that he was behind in his class assignments and not understanding the material. I asked him if he had talked to the professor. "No." I asked him if he was getting tutoring help. "No. I cannot do that. That's for students who are struggling." I asked him if he was sharing his stress and concerns with one of our campus psychologists. "No. I could never share my feelings with a stranger like that."

Ultimately, I was able to convince the student over time that he needed to be doing all three. His stress lowered thanks to his talking once a week with our psychologist. He was able to speak with the professor regularly and better understand why he was not mastering the material. Small and large group tutoring sessions helped him to solidify the material so that he truly learned it for the exams.

The point is: do not be stubborn. Ask for help. There is a well filled with services, available at your university, to help you get through the experience.

#11-Guilt is Normal—One of the difficult life changes that occurs when you are in med school is that a new emotional reality sets in. You will feel guilt creeping over you so that it blankets your life for much of your time in med school.

For example, when you are studying, you will feel guilty that you cannot spend time with those important in your life. When you are spending time away from school to be with your loved ones, friends, and/or family, you will feel guilty for not studying.

If you are married, you will feel guilty that you are not able to spend more time with your spouse. If you are a parent, you will feel guilty that you are not spending enough time with your child/children. You will also feel guilty that your spouse/partner is doing more of the work to support and manage your child/children and your home.

Your friendships will change. You will feel guilty when all your friends are out together, and you can't go because you have an exam coming up.

The feelings of guilt are normal. Know that you are not the only person struggling with that invisible shroud of false culpability. Most of your classmates will struggle with the same issue. The good news is you are not alone, though few may speak of what it feels like. Unfortunately, there is no antidote to feelings of guilt. You just must get used to feeling that way and convince your head and your heart that this is a temporary reality.

#12-Your Relationships Will (Need to) Fundamentally Change—Just as you will experience feelings of guilt for not being able to invest in your family and friends, so, too, will your relationships fundamentally change because of med school. Although you may not want them to change, they may need to in order for you to get through this period of your life.

You will not have the energy and time to invest in your family and friends like you did in high school and undergrad; you will have less time and energy to invest. Therefore, it will be important for you to sit your family and friends down before you leave and have a heart-to-heart discussion about how your relationship with them will have to change.

You won't have time to answer 43 texts a day from your mom or best friend. If every moment you receive a text message you turn your attention away from your study time, you will not get the necessary hours of studying completed that you need to achieve. Having a conversation with mom and dad about the need to change your communication level with them will be important and will avoid hurt feelings and concern.

You won't have as much time to go out with your friends, either, if they are in the area. Fewer nights having fun together will leave them wondering why you aren't as devoted a friend. Because most of your friends may not be in med school, they will likely fail to understand why you are no longer dedicating time and energy to the friendship. A conversation before you leave can help avoid hurt feelings between friends. Note that periodic reminders may be necessary.

Finally, if you are married, the nature of your relationship with your spouse will almost certainly be altered. You are going to have less time to be spontaneous and will more than likely have to begin scheduling time to be with your partner.

By scheduling, you guarantee that time will exist for you to be with him/her. If you don't schedule a block for him/her, it won't happen. I highly recommend you have a conversation with your spouse/partner about how you try to maintain good communication, prioritize time together, and maintain intimacy within your relationship. It will be time well spent and will be a conversation you can check back into at varying intervals during this experience.

#13-Humility is Your Friend—Everyone remembers that jackass personality that you went to high school or college with. No one likes jackasses. When I use that terminology, I am describing that man/woman you know who is a cocky, know-it-all, abrasive, and pretentious ass.

I will be honest with you that there are many physicians who display both arrogant and hyper-inflated egos. Sometimes, rather than this experience humbling an individual, it has the opposite effect: the person graduates med school with a God Complex the size of Montana.

No one enjoys working with someone like this. And I adamantly promise you no one will enjoy going to school with such a person. Last fall, I was standing in front of a new class of 432 students and I asked them who had a God complex. One student raised his hand. And, of course, I couldn't resist taking him on in front of his classmates. I asked him if he genuinely believed he knew more than everyone in the room. He nodded. I was dumbstruck. (Parenthetically, just so you know, about four months later he was in my office for having failed one of our courses. Needless to say, he did not claim to know more than the rest of his classmates anymore.)

If you are the type of personality who leans toward God complex, be prepared to be knocked off your pedestal in med school. The process is a great opportunity to learn how to be humble and how to serve others, using medicine as your tool.

Dr. Mike Johnston, a dear friend and colleague in Kansas City, has been a physician for almost 50 years and is the best representation, I know, of how to be a great physician, but an even better human being. He is caring, empathic, kind, smart, professional, and humble. Yet he in no manner flouts his intellect. He would never assume to be better than anyone else he works with or treats as a patient. And he treats every patient who comes through his door as the most important patient he will see that day. When I think of a humble and gifted physician, I think of him.

Strike out every day to be a Dr. Mike Johnston; caring, empathetic, kind, smart, professional, and humble. If you can do that every day of your career in-and-out of medical school, you will be in a very good place professionally.

#14-For At Least Half of Your Class, Your Grades Will Not be A's—I do not share this with you to scare you. I share this with you to just be honest about the statistical realities of med school and to reinforce with you that not making the dean's list is okay.

The fact is that for many of you, this will be the first time in your life when you receive a grade of B, C, or F. And for some of you, this may initially be viewed as an earth-shattering reality. You all are great students, and many of you have had straight A grades from the first grade to the present. The likelihood of that continuing is low. Let me explain why.

See the bell curve below. First notice how many students receive A grades. It is quite a low number. The vast majority of the class will receive B-and-C-grades, with a percentage receiving a failing grade (Note: In most medical schools, a failing grade is a grade of 69% or lower). In the illustration below, students with grades left of 70% will be failing the exam.

The good news is that in most schools they do curve, or scale, your grades. Each school sets the curve at a different point. This is something you will want to understand very clearly before your take your first exam. Again, listen carefully in orientation.

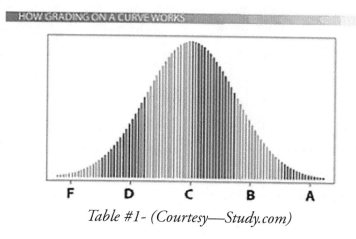

Table #1- (Courtesy—Study.com)

The bottom line is that you need to be emotionally and cognitively prepared that your grades will shift downward, and that is ok. You need to set your own goals from a grade perspective. I have seen plenty of great physicians with B and C GPAs. You know what they call the person who finished last in their medical school class? Doctor. So be honest with yourself in terms of your own personal grade expectations, set goals, and reach for those goals!

#15-Respect Each Other, Yourselves, and the Profession— When you graduate part of the ceremony will include your taking an oath to your profession. Part of that oath intimates that you will respect your role as a physician. One of the important responsibilities you have from the moment you enter is the responsibility of respect for your classmates, yourself and, ultimately, what it means to be a physician.

Being a physician means that you are a part of one of the most respected professions on earth. This designation carries great responsibility with it. So one of the things that I impress upon young med students is that in order to act the part of the physician you have an obligation to: 1) demonstrate respect to your classmates on a consistent basis; 2) respect yourself enough to act as if you are a doctor, which means always carrying yourself professionally when you are in public; and, 3) respect the medical profession and all it has to offer to you.

Acting like a physician may mean you should no longer act as you did when you were an undergraduate. You are no longer a "student" per se, you are a physician in training. When you are at the bar or in a restaurant, the grocery store, and/or the movie theatre, you must conduct yourself as if one of your patients is in the room with you. Carry yourself with a humble sense of quiet veneration. I will share more on professionalism in an upcoming chapter.

I have hundreds of stories of med students forgetting to respect each other and many more about med students who forgot what it meant to demonstrate respect towards the profession. I have had students arrested for DUIs, shoplifting, assault, and stalking. I have also had students show contempt and disrespect to classmate's actions which were so egregious that they were dismissed from school.

Do not fall into those embarrassingly dysfunctional traps. Each day, when you wake up to go to campus, think about the reasons why you wanted to be a physician. That usually is an altruistic reminder of why respect should become a cornerstone of your medical school experience.

#16-Practice Grit and Resilience—I mentioned earlier in this book the importance of developing grit and resilience in order to make it through this experience. Grit and resilience are learned skills that you will have to practice regularly in order to hone a skill and reap its benefits to the benefit of your future patients.

Without effective coping skills, one simply cannot make it through this experience. So how are you going to cope

STRAIGHT TALK FOR MEDICAL STUDENTS

appropriately? How will you know when you need to take a break, suck it up, or let a negative experience roll off your back? I can't emphasize how important it will be for you to develop good, effective coping skills.

If you are worried that you may not have the grit and resilience to make it through school, you may want to reach out to a counselor or therapist to talk about the reasons why you are struggling in this important area of competency, as this will be something you need to develop not only for med school, but for life as well.

#17-Your Old Way of Studying Won't Be Sufficient in Medical School—By the time one receives a diploma from an undergraduate program, you have developed a certain set of study skills and habits. In my experience, for most med students, the study skillset they bring with them from their undergraduate programs is not sufficient enough to ensure success at the medical school level. This means you will need to rethink how you study and do it quickly, so you don't fall behind.

Most students who leave undergrad and go on to med school did not have to work very hard to achieve A and B grades. Most students at the undergraduate level use repetition and memorization as their main tool for exam preparation. There are two problems with this approach in med school: 1) the volume of information you have to review and learn is simply too great in size to be memorized; and, 2) you will really need to synthesize and learn to master the information for the long-term. Because much of this information will be on your board examinations, you will need to learn it both for the subject matter exam that you are taking in years one and two and the licensing exam you will take at the end of years two and three. Memorizing for the short-term doesn't work.

Learning research tells us that if a student is able to review material 5 times prior to the exam, that they are far more likely to retain the information. Most learning specialists encourage students to set up a study plan that includes daily reviews of course content they have previously reviewed. The multiple review process helps you to initially learn the information over time and return to older information to ensure you are reviewing on multiple occasions prior to each exam.

When you arrive, schedule a meeting with one of the learning specialists, on-campus to talk about two important learning strategies: 1) creating your study plan for each day and week of a course; and, 2) create your material review process so that you will have a clear understanding of how to review the material multiple times (i.e. 5 times) prior to testing.

#18-Don't Be a Filthy Animal—This piece of advice may have you scratching your head. The fact is that there are two patterns of behavior demonstrated by medical students that have something to do with being a "filthy animal".

First, med students get so busy studying and going to class and lab that after being enrolled for several months, they stop caring about their personal hygiene. They shower less frequently, and that leads to smelly students. Each academic year, I have to sit down face-to-face with 2 or 3 students to have a conversation about personal hygiene and how that relates to professionalism. It's an awkward conversation, but I would much rather have it with them in year one than get a call from a clerkship preceptor who is questioning their professionalism while they are in a clinical setting. Being a slob may have been "cool" in undergrad. It's not "cool" in med school. The bottom line is that personal hygiene is one of those life priorities that need to be exercised every day. Shower. Wash your laundry and lab coat. Your classmates will thank you.

Second, there is a pattern of behavior that seems exclusive to the male population of each class, as the women refrain from engaging in this type of behavior. Every year, there is a small number of male classmates who have little to no experience having relationships with women. They may desire to but simply can't seem to manage their communication with females well.

I had a first-year medical student who matriculated at the University. He was very smart and did really well academically in his first couple of classes. Then the complaints began coming into my office about him. All were from women in his class who said that he had no boundaries in his communication with them. He would call. He would text over and over again. He would ask them out on dates. Most of them tried to handle the situation with care, not wishing to hurt his feelings, but when his solicitations did not stop, they were forced to be very blunt with him telling him to cease communicating with them. He failed to heed their requests, and they became afraid of him.

The situation went on with multiple students and endured over a lengthy period. I met with him and spoke directly about the problems and told him to stop contacting the women who had complained. His focus just shifted to another, new woman in his class. I finally met with him and took disciplinary action against him and required him to stop all contact with female classmates which was non-curriculum related. That finally worked. But then he started going off campus and contacting local women…who ultimately contacted my office with complaints about what they perceived as his stalking them.

What's the moral of this story? First, no means no. If a female student requests that you stop contacting her, honor the request and move on. Second, you don't want to get a reputation for being a stalker. Third, you are here to learn how to become a physician, not Casanova. Focus on the reason why you are here and keep your eye on the prize, rather than turning into a Tinder maniac who won't take no for an answer. That means, don't be creepy.

#19-If You Do Your Part, You Will Have a Job at the End of This—It is a fact that there are more medical students graduating than there are residency spots available. I could write an entire chapter as to why this is the case, but I won't. That said, throughout my entire career, I cannot think of one student who did their part to get to graduation who didn't ultimately match.

Faculty like to hang residency match over your head like it is a black cloud of doom and gloom, when in fact, it isn't. Here's why: 1) we have an unprecedented shortage of good physicians and healthcare workers; 2) hospital systems are needing to fill gaps in their systems, in other words, they are hiring as fast as they can; and, 3) universities are graduating, for the most part, competent student doctors who will be a great fit for that need.

What is you part? 1) study hard; 2) don't fail any med school classes; and 3) don't fail any national licensing exams. If you are able to do this, you will have a residency/job when you graduate.

Now, will that mean if you have straight C's in med school, you are going to get that oft-coveted Dermatology residency? Absolutely not. You need to be realistic in terms of your capabilities versus your expectations and you need to pay attention to what GPA as well as what board exam score you need to have in order to secure a residency spot in a particular specialty.

When I look back on the students who struggled to match they share a common set of variables: 1) they had multiple course failures; 2) they failed one or more attempts at their national licensing exams; and/or, 3) They did not have a realistic understanding of what specialty to apply for, given their academic record. In other words, they applied for a specialty that would never accept their grades and/or licensing exam scores.

The bottom line is that the nay-sayers and doom and gloom prognosticators are wrong about 95% of the time. Ignore their negativity, keep working hard, and be realistic. If you are able to do those things, you will have both a residency spot and career awaiting you. Good luck!

#20-Common Mistakes by Medical Students That Drive Me Crazy—As a medical school insider who has seen just about everything in my career, these are the pet peeves that really tick me off. Do NOT attempt to do any of the following:

- **Cheating**—This is self-explanatory. And yet every year, there is a medical student who feels so desperate that he/she chooses to cheat during an exam. I have seen it all: a) hidden cell phone in the bathroom trash can during an exam; b) tiny writing, in pencil, on the keyboard of the student's ipad; c) hidden text books in the ceiling of the bathroom; and, d) two friends, sitting side-by-side reading off each other's exam screens.

    You have worked far too hard to get where you presently are to have it all thrown away by attempting to cheat on an exam. It just isn't worth it. Because at the schools I have worked at, cheating is a dismissible offense.

- **Stimulant Usage**—Using a controlled substance that requires a physician's prescription to gain an advantage over your classmates is a big no-no. Not only is it cheating, it's also a huge concern given the fact that if you become a physician you will be responsible for writing prescriptions yourself. This is one that always gets you dismissed from school.

- **Disrespect to Support Staff**—If you want to see an angry Dr. Winslow, be disrespectful to one of the support staff that works on-campus. I have had several students do this over the years. They think that just because someone cleans the bathrooms or mows the grass that they are beneath them. This couldn't be further from the truth. If you are disrespectful to staff at the university, you will be disrespectful to nurses, med techs, etc. Don't start this habit. Nip it in the bud.

- **Don't Carry Your Vomit Bag in the Car with You**—I once had a student call our office, stating that she was sick with the flu and needed to go to the Emergency Room. She said that she didn't have a car and could we arrange for a ride for her. One of my staff, Catherine, was nice enough to volunteer. She drove to the student's apartment, picked her up and when she got into the car, she was carrying a double lined, plastic Walmart bag full of vomit. She wanted to bring the vomit with her in case the ER physician wanted to test the puke.

    Just because you are in med school does not guarantee that you have good common sense. Believe it or not, an ER doctor is not going to test your vomit for any reason. Leave the throw-up at home. That will eliminate the risk of that Walmart bag splitting open and dropping flu vomit all over the inside of a very nice person's car!

- **Over-Involving Your Parents**—When you come to medical school, we assume you are an adult. And an adult does not call mom and dad whenever he/she has a situation that stresses them out.

I get far too many calls from parents wanting to know details about their son's/daughter's academic life. First, I cannot talk to them because Federal Law (FERPA) precludes me from doing so. Second, I shouldn't be talking to them, I should be talking to you. Don't send your parents to do your job.

Over the last two years, I have developed a great sense of respect for one of my students. She struggled off and on academically and came to me for help to get her back on track. The staff pulled together and really helped her out. Plus, she worked really hard. But her mother, who loves her very, very much, began calling me and would not stop.

It became a burden after a while. Calls continued month after month. The mom cried repeatedly. I kept reassuring her that her daughter was going to be ok. But what I figured out after a while is that she was calling me to be her therapist (which I am most definitely not). I finally had to cut the calls off, and I had to meet with the student to tell her clearly that I was not here to be her mom's support system. It was a difficult conversation, but the student understood completely. By the way, the student ended up just fine and graduates this spring.

My hope is that you will take this advice seriously. It comes from a good place, in that my hope is that if you are steered away from some of the common pitfalls, you can avoid problems that may suck time, energy, and pleasure from you during a semester when time is a luxury. Remember, be honest with yourself, open to advice, and be proactive in seeking help.

CHAPTER 8

Mastering Professionalism in Medical School

Over the last two years, medical education has seen a spike in the number of articles written by colleagues about the need to see better, more comprehensive training, for medical students in the area of professionalism. This call within the profession comes at a time when medical education and healthcare in general are more politicized, criticized, and complex than ever before.

What does this mean for you? Well, at the outset you need to be prepared to recognize professionalism as one of the main tenets of your medical education. And that will require you to understand what professionalism means, how the medical world defines professionalism in terms of your obligations as a future physician, and how you will infuse professionalism into your own training.

In the past it was believed that a sense of professionalism was handed from one generation to the next through the amorphous almost osmotic responsibility of role-modeling. That, however, is no longer the case given the manner in which the present-day healthcare delivery system has doctors tied to electronic medical records and to seeing a specified number of patients each day. That has left medical education holding the bag on how best to inculcate the quality of professionalism to medical students.

Be prepared to be exposed to some conversations about professionalism and how you plan to live the concept into your own personal and professional life. Most medical students arrive at med school with a basic understanding of what it means to be professional but lack the details that can only be obtained through experiencing medical school and clinical rotations.

Defining Professionalism

The Latin word, "professio", meaning public declaration, is the word from which professionalism was derived. Today's modern definition has become modified somewhat to apply to medicine more directly.

Michael Lacombe (2007), a physician whose own writings about professionalism sparked additional conversation, defined a professional physician as the following: "I knew a doctor once who was honest, but gentle with his honesty, and was loving, but careful with his love, who was disciplined without being rigid, and right without the stain of arrogance, who was self-questioning without self-doubt, introspective and reflective and in the same moment, decisive, who was strong, hard, adamant, but all these things laced with tenderness and understanding, a doctor who worshipped his calling without worshipping himself, who was busy beyond belief, but who had time—time to smile, to chat, to touch the shoulder and take the hand, and who had time enough for death as well as life. Now *there* is a professional."

Given the fact that professionalism can be seen as an ethos, a cultural trend, or as a set of clearly defined attributes or components that must be learned. We can really divide a modern definition of professionalism into three separate ideas: 1) a generalized definition that focuses on the competence or skill expected of said professional, 2) more specific to medicine, excellence in medical practice, and, 3) a definition denoting meeting certain professional standard/attributes set forth by a group or governing body within medicine, with the expectation that the professional will master said attributes.

Components of Professionalism

It is much easier, from a pedagogical perspective, to determine a set of components or attributes by which to measure one's professionalism. Most medical students' attitudes about becoming a professional lean toward, and I am paraphrasing, "Tell me and show me how to be a professional and I will do what you tell me to do..."

Several academics and professional organizations, who specialize in medical education, have attempted to denote the standards or competencies that should be a part of the definition of professionalism in medicine starting with the following by the Accreditation Council of Graduate Medical Education (ACGME):

1) Demonstrating Professional Conduct and Accountability.
2) Demonstrating Humanism and Cultural Proficiency.
3) Maintaining Emotional, Physical, and Mental Health, and Pursuing Continual Personal and Professional Growth.

(ACGME, 2017)

One of the institutions I worked at developed a professionalism rubric used to grade students, faculty, and staff professionalism. The definition was separated into three categories with specific definitions for how that category was lived out in day-to-day practice:

- **Humanistic Behavior**—Includes respect, compassion, probity, honesty, and trustworthiness.

- **Accountability**—Demonstrates accountability to patients, society, and the profession, including the duty to act in response to the knowledge of professional behavior of others.

- **Ethics**—Demonstrates knowledge of and the ability to apply ethical principles, in the practice and research of medicine, particularly in the areas of provision or withholding of clinical care, confidentiality of patient information, informed consent, business practices, the conduct of research, and the reporting of research results.

(Kansas City University, 2019)

Finally, as a third example of applying a definition to the day-to-day work of a student doctor or a practicing physician, Stanford University's School of Medicine has created a list of 12 Objectives and Expectations for their students, faculty, and staff as it pertains to professionalism:

1) Adheres to Stanford School of Medicine and Stanford Hospital policies.

2) Arrives on time and prepared for educational and patient expectations.

3) Fulfills obligations and commitments in timely fashion.

4) Respectfully and tactfully questions policies, procedures, and practices perceived as unfair.

5) Takes responsibility for shortcoming and areas for improvement.

6) Recognizes errors and impairments in peers and reports these to appropriate entities.

7) Maintains personal control amidst adverse or trying circumstances.

8) Takes initiative, perseveres, and is able to prioritize and to manage time.

9) Takes on appropriate share of teamwork.

10) Reports accurately and fully on patient care activities.

11) Always ensures transfer of responsibility for patient care.

12) Informs supervisor/team when mistakes occur or when faced with a conflict of interest.

If we take these three examples of how various academicians and universities are defining the components of professionalism, I believe we get a pretty clear understanding of not only the definition of professionalism, but also how professionalism is contextually practiced in a medical education and clinical environment, as well.

I would encourage you to read over these attributes and familiarize yourself with them, as I promise you these will be valuable context for any future conversations you have about professionalism.

Learning Professionalism in Medical School

Understanding the meaning of professionalism is, in a medical context, one thing. Understanding the components and attributes of professionalism is something different. Gaining insight into how a definition is fully implemented, can only come with the full process of classroom teaching and clinical experience in working with patients.

Historically, the most effective way of teaching professionalism was through didactic educating within the classroom, together with mentoring from experienced physicians directly to students. Unfortunately, that older, effective model has faded away and although students have the classroom experience, the opportunities for mentoring have grown fewer and further between.

How are medical students being educated in professionalism today at some of the nation's best schools? Most well positioned universities understand, first and foremost, that they must create a safe environment in which conversations about professionalism can occur. Without a safe environment, faculty, staff and students will not "open up" in critical "experienced-based" conversations.

It seems that most schools understand the need for a classroom component that highlights the following opportunities:

- **Self-Awareness and Introspection**—This may include workshops and classroom conversations about self-awareness and introspection. These are focused on getting you to understand that each student has strengths and weaknesses within the realm of professionalism and helping to identify one's own strengths and weaknesses.

- **Student Facilitated Workshops**—These workshops are focused on using real-life scenarios to highlight physicians acting unprofessionally. Role-playing can assist students in understanding the nuances of professionalism in a clinical setting.

- **Feedback Skills Workshops**—Empowers students to effectively speak up and converse with peers and superiors on professionalism-related topics.

Contrary to the above, however, several schools are not moving away from the idea that mentoring between faculty and staff to students is a critically important component to teaching professionalism. Schools are intentionally setting up advising and other types of programs that require students to interact with faculty members on a regular basis. Research conducted over many decades supports this approach, because the research highlights that if students at the undergraduate and graduate levels can develop a meaningful mentoring relationship with a faculty or staff member, they are more likely to be academically successful and mirror increased attributes of professionalism.

I would encourage every medical student to take the time to get to know one of your faculty members during your time in the school of medicine. That could be your advisor, one of your favorite faculty members, or a staff member in student affairs. Meet with them regularly. Talk about your experiences. Begin to notice how they conduct themselves on-campus. This may help you to learn how you wish to conduct yourself once you are on clinical rotations and move into residency.

Common Professionalism Pitfalls

There are certainly varying degrees of unprofessionalism. From minor offenses that require a conversation between faculty member and student, to those that might fall in a more serious category, each unprofessional behavior certainly has a story behind it.

I will share one anecdote that received national press attention in 2019. A newly minted doctor went out with her friends drinking in a bar district in Miami. She was clearly drunk when she hailed an Uber to come pick her up. When the car arrived, the driver realized how drunk she was and refused to drive her to her destination. She lost control and not only verbally abused him but also unloaded personal items out of his car all over the street corner at which he had stopped.

What she didn't realize was that she was being video recorded the entire time she was yelling, screaming, and cussing. The video went viral. And within a week, she was fired from her residency. Her firing had nothing to do with her abilities as a physician. It had everything to do with unprofessional behavior. Most people say of professional behavior, "I know it when I see it…" In this case, most people knew her behavior was highly unprofessional because they saw it right there in a viral video.

This is where I get a bit paternal. Don't allow yourself to fall into the trap of unprofessional behavior over a night of alcohol that can cost you your career. Again, you have worked way too hard to get to this point. Don't blow it over something stupid.

As a higher education insider, I have seen many examples of unprofessional behavior by students. Here are the most common examples that seem to happen annually:

- **Nights Out with Friends**—A night out with friends can result in bad consequences; a police arrest for driving under the influence; a shoplifting arrest for shopping while drunk; a complaint from a member of the opposite sex claiming that you were "creepy and handsy". All are real-life results of what seemed like an innocent night out for fun. I am not saying you shouldn't ever go out with friends...but I am saying that when you are out, remain in control.

- **Emailing Professors**—This is the most common professionalism infraction. A student doesn't like a decision by a professor. The student emails the professor when they are angry. The professor reads the email and notices both the tone and tenor of the email and subsequently calls the student affairs office wanting disciplinary action taken against the student.

  Do not permit a thoughtless email to a professor to trip you up. The number one rule of thumb should be do not email anyone when you are angry. Second, you should have a friend or family member review the email before you send it.

- **Dating Relationships in Med School**—These are totally acceptable as long as the beginning, middle and end of the relationship maintain respectful professional boundaries, both on and off-campus. I have had students arrested for standing outside their girlfriend's apartment, screaming at her at the top of his lungs. I have had students file complaints against their former girlfriend because she became violent and punched and kicked her partner.

Relationships and how those are projected publicly should be positive things, not things that cause you harm in terms of your reputation. Keep that in mind as you and your significant other navigate issues together.

- **Inappropriate Dress**—I have had students show up to class in inappropriate outfits (remember this isn't under-grad). I have had a student show up to a disciplinary hearing in his pajamas. That episode did not end well for him. I have, as well, had students dress inappropriately at off-campus social events. The bottom line is that you project who you are to the world. Don't let your fashion choices cause people to doubt who you are and what you are capable of from a professional perspective.

- **Personal Conversations at Work**—About once a year, I receive a call from a clinical clerkship coordinator with a story of one of our students saying something that crossed a professional boundary, such as jokes that aren't appropriate; asking a nurse out on a date; making references to one's sex life. All have been communication lines of good taste and professional conduct that students have crossed in the recent past.

If you would be embarrassed to have a particular conversation with your own grandmother is a good measuring stick for keeping quiet. If the answer is yes, and you would be embarrassed by the conversation, then don't bring it up at work.

Mastering Professionalism

The mark of a truly professional student may be best described by saying that they act professionally even when there are no faculty and staff around. Is that the kind of medical student you will eventually become? I hope so, because it will ultimately set you up for success in both your clinical rotations in years 3 and 4, but also in your residency following graduation.

Mastering professionalism includes several key tenets we have touched on within this chapter:

- Attending all professionalism trainings.
- Understanding the core components that make up professionalism in medicine and how those apply to your day-to-day work as a physician.
- Being open to feedback and becoming self-aware of one's own shortcomings.
- Learning and practicing how to have difficult conversations with classmates, professors, and patients.
- Reaching out to faculty and staff regularly in an attempt to cultivate a mentoring relationship.
- Avoiding common mistakes made by med students.

If you are able to accomplish these steps while you are a first- and second-year medical student, you will be ready to demonstrate your professionalism in your clinical years and beyond. Good luck...this is something you can do easily!

CHAPTER 9

Preparing for Year Two

I know, you haven't even started year one, why am I bringing up your second year as a med student? Well, either I want to annoy you to no end, or there just may be a bit of practical advice about transitioning from year one to year two that might be worth knowing.

First and foremost, I hope you will give yourself some time to truly celebrate your successful navigation of year one! Woo-hoo!

Once you have finished celebrating and relaxing a little bit, however, it is time to begin thinking about the future and what you need to be thinking about as a sophomore. You aren't going to find a lot written about year two of med school, so I think it is important that I hit on a few key ideas that may get you headed in the right direction for year two.

What is Important About Year Two?

In year one you gained an understanding of the didactic foundation for anatomy, biochemistry, genetics, physiology, neuroscience, etc. In many ways, you have absorbed the basic science in each of these subject areas. The good news is that you have developed a strong foundation about each of these subjects. Now it is time to integrate the various segments of subject matter together.

Some schools study the healthy systems in year one and then study the same systems but examine the pathology of those systems in year two. For other schools, they use case-based learning to examine the basic scientific understanding of the systems and then look further at the systems in year two using the case-based approach. Each school is somewhat different, but you should expect that year two will require you to work even harder and to deal with more complex understandings of what you learned in year one.

The other common theme you will experience in year two is taking the basic science foundation you learned earlier and connecting it very directly to the clinical setting. In other words, you are moving from "classroom to bedside…" according to Dr. Joshua Nosanchuck.

Finally, the biggest difference between year one and year two will be the fact that a large chunk of year two will be spent preparing for your board examination (USMLE and/ or COMLEX) which will take place late spring, early in the following summer.

The Sophomore Slump

Why isn't much communicated about the sophomore year of medical school? That's a valid question, because it is an important time in a med student's life, as they typically experience a letdown of sorts as they enter the second year. The **Sophomore Slump**, as it is referred to by those who have seen generations of students, can be a valid phenomenon, that we frequently see on campuses. This slump usually signifies a decrease in students' commitment to their schoolwork, lowered enthusiasm towards their overall med school experience, and what might be termed a general malaise.

Many theories exist as to why the sophomore slump is a real trend. Some of the reasons include the following:

1) **Loss of "Specialness"**—I do believe that colleges/ universities spend so much time and energy focusing on first year med students that when that first year is successfully completed, they tend to no longer make second-year students feel as special. All that attention they received in year one vanishes out the door. Sophomore medical students return to campus for year two and are taken aback by the lack of staff focus on their class. They go through a ten-day orientation as new students and a three-hour orientation as second year students. I have had many sophomores say something to the effect of, "Does the university even know I exist anymore? It's like you guys don't care about me". The

185

best universities take intentional steps to ensure that every class feels as if they have the university's overall attention, but the loss of specialness is a real thing.

2) **More Difficult Coursework**—Sophomore students may be realizing that their coursework is growing more complex, not to mention the fact that they have to prepare for their first licensing board examination at the end of the year, they are adding board study onto an already maxed-out study plan.

3) **Second Year Med Students Are Held to Higher Standard**—Because sophomores have been in med school for a year, an assumption is made that they know what to do and how to do it. They are held to a higher standard and receive less benefit of the doubt.

4) **Less Excitement**—Let's face it: A bit of ho-hum sets in after you have been doing something for a year, and students do fall into the trap of taking med school for granted. It's generally less exciting the second time you try something. That goes for med school, too.

Why is it important that universities give thought and focus to sophomore students? First, the second highest attrition rate on most campuses is the second-year cohort. First year medical students make up the highest rate of attrition, while sophomores are the second highest. From an institutional perspective, it makes good sense to focus on sophomores and ensure that they survive year two as successfully as the first. In fact, the vast majority of attrition at medical schools happens in years one and two. Very few third- and fourth-year medical students drop out of or fail med school.

The definition of the term *sophomore* is "*wise fool*". In this case, you may be labeled wise fools because sophomores tend to think they know everything about surviving when in fact most haven't figured it all out just yet. You still have work to do to hone your study skills, to begin board exam planning, to begin thinking about what specialty you may be interested in, and to navigating the complex next steps in the curriculum. You will have made progress but aren't fully formed, yet.

That's why I want to take a bit of time with you to highlight a few key factors for second year success, what steps you need to take to be ready to go back to medical school following those the small amount of time you have off, and what internal conversations you need to have with yourself to get you focused on year two.

Signs of the Sophomore Slump

Just what symptoms should you look for that are indicative of the sophomore slump? Beware of the following behaviors/outcomes:

- **You Don't Want to Go Back to Med School**—If you had a successful first year in med school, you should be at least positive about the prospect of going back, re-connecting with your med school friends, and re-engaging your brain.

- **You Are Calling, Texting, and Emailing Family Too Much**—You find yourself calling to complain about how you simply don't want to be at med school right now. This sense of malaise indicates something is wrong. You have already completed a year of this. There is typically less homesickness in the sophomore year, so this could be a sign that something is wrong.

- **You Find That Your Motivation Has Dropped Significantly**—You are telling yourself that on a scale of 1-10, your motivation was an eight during your first year, yet has now dropped to a three.

- **Sudden and Significant Drop in Grades**—If you were a B student during your first year and you start getting failing grades, something is seriously wrong. This could be associated with more complex subject matter, however, a sudden drop in grades which seems unexplained, may be an indication that something is seriously wrong.

- **You Communicate Disappointment with Your Med School Experience**—If you were enthusiastic last year and this year, you appear to be backtracking on feeling this is the right place for you, this could be a sign something is amiss.

- **You Express Confusion About the Future**. "I don't know what specialty I want to do...", "I have no idea why I am here...", or "I just don't know who I am anymore..." are all expressions of feeling out of sorts with your experience and typical among second year students.

Let us imagine that you are hearing and recognizing one or several signs of the Sophomore Slump. What can you do to make sure that you proactively address this malaise before too much time passes and you cannot academically recover from the let down? Consider taking these steps:

- **Talk to Someone You Trust Proactively**—It can be a classmate, a parent(s), your advisor, a counselor, a staff member in student affairs, just someone you trust. This conversation could include a post-mortem on year one, what worked and didn't work, what you are excited about in year two, and what your goals are for the year. Being honest with yourself about the fact that it won't feel as nerve racking, exciting, and new is critical to do.

- **This is Normal**—It's okay if you feel this sense of incompleteness about your second year. A large percentage of students do. Be patient with yourself and don't fret as you wrestle with these new feelings. Refocusing yourself on the goals you laid out for year two may help shift your focus from the slumping feelings to something more exciting.

- **Be Positive**—You are skilled about what it means to be a student at your university. You know where everything resides. You have taken courses successfully. You completed year one of medical school! You have a group of friends who are going to be excited to see you. You know the ropes. Embrace all of those positive facts.

- **Explore the Dissatisfaction**—Don't be afraid to dig deeper as to the "why" of your dissatisfaction. Is it nerves? Is it the prospect of seemingly unending and more difficult coursework? Could it be a social issue? Are you stretched too thin with student organization commitments? Ask questions and really work to open up about what you are feeling.

- **Ask for Help**—The bottom line is that if you continue to struggle, reach out for help. Remember that there are a substantial number of experts on-campus who are trained to help you work through this second-year slump.

Important Things to Do Leading Up to Year Two

As you head towards year two, there are a few practical things you will want to put on your to-do list in order to be proactive and ready. I would suggest you do the following before you return to campus for year two:

1) **Take Time to Relax**—Go on a vacation and do whatever relaxes you. This could be with family or a significant other. Just take someone along with you

that you like to be around, as your time off is limited and you will want to make sure you maximize your recovery from year one with someone who understands what you have been through.

2) **Goal Setting**—On a piece of paper jot down no more than 5 goals you want to accomplish in year two. At least one of these should be a personal, rather than a professional goal. What are your goals for grades? What leadership roles do you want to assume? What community service do you with to become involved within?

3) **Update Your CV**—The time between first and second year is the perfect time to update your CV. If you do this at the end of each year, you won't have to go back in year four and try and remember all you accomplished. It will be all right there, ready when you need it. These updates could include community service you completed, leadership positions you assumed, and/or research you participated in during year one.

4) **Assess Your Sophomore Slump Feelings**—Go back in this book to the page where we outline the signs of the sophomore slump. Are you feeling any of those things? Take time to assess what you are feeling about going back to med school for year two. If you are feeling hesitation about going back, talk it through with someone you trust.

5) **Identify Your Course Content Proficiency**—Review your courses from year one. What subject matter are you strong in and what subject matter areas do you sense weakness? You will want to identify this, as the process will help inform what you should spend more time on in your board prep studying. For example, if you are great in biochemistry, but struggled in physiology, you will want to dedicate more study time to boning up on physiology during you board preparations.

6) **Create a Board Prep Plan**—Go online and look at board prep plans created by a variety of medical students. Then set up an appointment to meet with one of the learning specialists. Ask them to advise you on how to create a study plan. They will give you their expert opinion on how to design a plan. Take their advice, and review what you learned from other students. Then finalize a plan for yourself. One piece of advice, you only need 6 to 8 weeks of intensive board prep time in order to be successful. According to research, studying intensely for three or four months is not only unnecessary but may have an adverse effect.

7) **Purchase Board Prep Materials**—Do your homework on what board resources to purchase. I will warn you that this has become what some might term a racket, as there are companies out there who will make millions off of selling unhelpful board prep materials to medical

students. Talk to your classmates. Read reviews online. What materials does your administration endorse? Take all of these into consideration before you purchase.

8) **Be Careful on Your Board Prep Timing**—In my experience, you will have plenty of time to prepare for boards. That said, the question that students always want answered is when they should start board preparations during the second year. There are two camps who have very different recommendations: 1) Start in the fall semester and read up on subject matter that you have traditionally been weak in and then start your formal prep beginning January of your second year. 2) Do not do board preparations in the fall, as it actually distracts you from doing well in your classes. Start your board prep in late February of your second year.

I cannot really tell you which works better. What I can tell you is that I have seen many second-year students who have failed second year courses because they were focused on studying for boards too early in the year. That is not something you want to do. So whatever plan you decide to implement, make sure you leave yourself ample study time for your coursework, otherwise you may be actually becoming counterproductive.

9) **Advise Your Family That You Are Going Radio Silent**—Before you head back to campus to start

second year, remind your family and close friends that life is about to change once again; that second year will tax you in new and unique ways and that you will be forced to return to the old rules from year one about staying in touch with them.

Closing Thoughts on Year Two

The sophomore year does not have to be a disappointing slog for you. If set up the right way, it can become an easy extension to the success you achieved during your first year. If you struggled in year one, it can be a new beginning and a refreshing journey so that you can make up for what was perhaps a less than stellar performance in the previous year.

The good news about the sophomore year is a) a sophomore slump happens to a minority of students; and, b) you are returning to campus already having a peer group of established relationships and friendships. You also know most of the professors you have had for courses already. So, the downside to the newness is no longer a liability. Instead, it has become an asset.

It is my belief that if you can talk openly and honestly about the slump and the potential for its onset, you are more prepared to deal with it should it occur to you. Remember, always, that you have already navigated the toughest year of your educational career. If you can get through the first year, successfully, everything else pales in comparison. You can do this!

CHAPTER 10

You Deserve to Be Here

We end almost where we began, in celebrating what an amazing accomplishment it is to want to be a physician. We have covered a lot of ground over the last 9 chapters and my hope is that you have learned a few things that will aid you in surviving year one of your experience and to prepare you for success in the remaining three years ahead.

These are concerning times. Just yesterday, New York City experienced the highest number of COVID 19 deaths, thus far, in this pandemic. And we have no idea how many deaths are yet to come. Who is it that is standing between all of us civilians and that prolific virus? Doctors and nurses and all the other people who are a dedicated part of the medical community. They have become world-wide heroes. They aren't sheltering in their own homes; rather they are at work, enduring endless 12-hour shifts to take care of the sick and dying, so the rest of us can play our own small parts in this unfolding drama in relative security.

And here you are…wanting to join the ranks of those heroes. Knowing all you know about the pandemic we have faced, the lightning spread of this latest disease, and yet you still want to be trained to be a physician. You are asking for the torch to be passed to you so that you can practice medicine and make a difference in the lives of your patients. That is both admirable and honorable.

There is one other first that might catch you off guard at one point or another in this medical school process. It is invisible and may actually become insidious at times. It may start during orientation or catch up to you in one of your first semester courses. It may even hit you during a clinical experience with a standardized patient. It will affect most of your classmates at one time or another. I am talking about imposter syndrome.

Imposter syndrome is a psychological state of mind that causes one to doubt his/her own skills and abilities, feel less intelligent than your peers, experience self-doubt, and possess a mindset of overall insecurity and uncertainty. It can also lead to burnout, an epidemic among medical students and physicians alike. It is a very real phenomenon. According to a research study published by the International Journal of Medical Education, 49% of women and 24% of men experienced some form of imposter syndrome during medical school.

One of the primary symptoms of burnout is the inability to positively recognize one's own accomplishments. You begin to see yourself as a fraud when it comes to what you are actually accomplishing. You begin to worry that your friends, your professors, and your mentor(s) will see you as a fraud, too.

Well, part of my job is to pick you up, remind you of how you got to this point in your life, and to give you the proverbial bitch slap to wake you up and help you move forward and throw the self-doubting in the trash bin.

If you want to avoid that snap-out-of-it slap from me, a friend, and/or a mentor, there are some practical things you can do to avoid self-doubt. First, each morning, take five seconds in front of the mirror in your bathroom to remind yourself of who you are and what your personal and professional identity is becoming to those who are around you on a daily basis. When you are standing in front of the mirror, I want you to do the following:

1) Remember back to your personal statement from your application and remind yourself what brought you to this place.

2) While you are remembering what got you to this place, visualize all you had to do to get here: your application, your secondary application, your interview, and your final acceptance. You did a lot of work to get to this point in your life. No one did it for you. You did it yourself.

3) And while you are standing there, I want you to look yourself in the eye and say one simple thing: "I deserve to be here…"

You do deserve to be here. And I am not B.S.-ing you. This is where some readers will roll their eyes and think about the idea of standing in front of the mirror and awkwardly talking to yourself. But I am here to tell you that there will be at least one moment over the next four years where you will need to stand in front of the mirror and remind yourself that you deserve to be in medical school.

Not to mention the fact that you did so much to get to this place. You went to college and did well enough in your science classes to be able to apply. No one did that for you. You completed the long application process, made the initial reviews, and were good enough to be invited to interview. No one gave you that opportunity. You earned it. And it was you who did well on your interview...well enough to be accepted. Your work and persistence earned you a place in your medical school class.

Sometimes, after one invests years of work into reaching a goal, they need a bit of a reminder that they did well and that their skills and abilities have worth that increase with each additional experience. Sometimes, of course, there will be moments when you are sitting in class, the professor calls on you and you will get the answer to the question badly wrong. That is an example of when the self-doubt may begin to creep in. Then some smart man or woman will sit up and answer the question and get it right and you will say to yourself, "Oh, my, god, how did she know the answer to that...I didn't even know what the concept the professor was referring to..."

Getting the question wrong is the first step to working harder to get the next question right. So instead of allowing the uncertainty and personal insecurity to seep into your mindset, remind yourself that you deserve to be here.

This is usually the moment when I make each section of the auditorium in orientation stand up and say, loudly and proudly, "I deserve to be here!" Then I remind them a few last thoughts. The first is that no one is expecting perfection from any student. Perfection is a delusion. Second, what we are expecting is that you will bring your best every day. And by bringing your best, we mean to come to class and lab ready to learn, possessing a growth mindset and a passion for why you are here. Third, I want you to think of the one person in your life who will be most proud to see you walk across the stage almost four years from now at graduation. Think of how proud that person will be. Do this for them. Motivate yourself for them. And shout it out, for them…I deserve to be here!

You deserve to be here.

References

American Association of Medical Colleges. (2020). *MCAT Frequently Asked Questions. www.aamc.org* .

American Association of Medical Colleges. (2019). *Physician Census. www.aamc.org* .

American Association of Medical Colleges. (2018). *Average Debt of Graduating Medical Students. www.aamc.org* .

American College Health Association. (2019). College Suicide Data. *www.acha.org* .

American Medical Association. (2019). *Physician Burnout: Improve Physician Satisfaction Outcomes. https://edhub. ama-assn.org/steps-forward/module/2702509* .

American Osteopathic Association. (2019). *Physician Census. www.aoa.org* .

American Psychological Association. (2019). *The Road to Resilience. www.apa.org* .

BMC Medical Education. (2019). *Physician Graduation Rates. www.bmcmedicaleducation.com.*

Council for Osteopathic Student Government Presidents. (2018). *Burnout and Depression Survery. www.aoa.org* .

Duckworth, A. (2016). *Grit: The Power of Passion and Perseverance.* Toronto, Ontario, Canada.

Health Careers. (2018). Minorities in Medicine: A Look at Physician Diversity. *www.healthcareers.com* .

Kansas City University of Medicine and Biosciences (2020). *Health and Technical Standards. www.kcumb.edu* .

Kansas City University of Medicine and Biosciences (2019). *Professionalism Rubric. www.kcumb.edu* .

Lacombe, M. (2007). *On Professionalism.* University of Alberta Health Sciences Journal, 4(1), p. 25-27.

Meeks, L., Case, B., and Herzer, K. (2019). *Change in Prevalence of Disabilities and Accommodation Practices Among US Medical Schools, 2016 vs. 2019.* Journal of American Medical Association, 322(20), p. 2022-2024.

Nama, N., MacPherson, P., Sampson, M., and McMillan, H.J. (2017). *Medical Students' Perception of LGBT Discrimination in Their Learning Environment and Their Self-Reported Comfort Level for Caring for LGBT Patients: A Survery Study.* Medical Education Online. 22(1).

Quek, T.T., Tam, W.W., Tran, B., Zhang, M., Chang, Z., Ho, C.S., and Ho, R.C. (2019). *The Global Prevalence of Anxiety Among Medical Students: A Meta-Analysis.* Journal of Environmental Research and Public Health. 16(15), 2735.

Schernhammer, Eva S.; Colditz, Graham A. (2004). *Suicide Rates Among Physicians: A Quantitative and Gender Assessment (Meta-Analysis).* American Journal of Psychiatry. **161** (12): 2295–2302.

Study.com. (2019). *Bell Curve: Definition & Impact on Grades.* *www.study.com* .

Twenge, Jean. *Generation Me.* Free Press, 2006.

Twenge, Jean. *iGen: Why Today's Super-Connected Kids are Growing Up Less Rebelious, More Tolerant, Less Happy-and Completely Unprepared for Adulthood.* Atria Books, 2017.

United States Department of Education. (2019). *Federal Financial Aid Data. www.ed.gov* .

Young, A., Chaudhry, H.J., Pei, X., Arnhart, K., Dugan, M., and Snyder, G.B (2017). *A Census of Actively Licensed Physicians in the United States.* American Medical Association.

About the Author

With 25 years of higher education experience, Dr. Richard Winslow has spent his career working with students at both the undergraduate and graduate levels at some of the nation's top colleges and universities. Dr. Winslow's innovative leadership in higher education has been noted in outlets such as **Forbes Magazine**, **Money Magazine**, **TIME Magazine**, and **US News and World Report**.

With significant experience in student services, enrollment management, and higher education consulting, Dr. Winslow's experience has led to significant successes.

His new *Straight Talk* series of books are meant to provide students and parents a guide to navigating college and medical school. You can access these books on Amazon and the consulting services he provides at: *www.richardpwinslow.com*

Richard received his bachelor's degree from William Jewell College in Kansas City and both his Master's and his Ph.D. from the University of Missouri-Kansas City.

Dr. Winslow lives in Kansas City with his wife, Dr. Jennifer Dennis, and their four sons, Barrett, Caleb, Liam, and Luke and their canine kids, Jack and Phoebe. In his spare time, Rick loves coaching little league baseball, playing the guitar, attending Kansas City Royals games with his kids, and spending time with his family and friends.

Check out Dr. Winslow's recent publication, *"Straight Talk for College Parents: An Insider's Guide to Helping Your Student Survive the First Year of College"*, at *www.amazon.com.*

NOTES

NOTES

NOTES

NOTES

Made in United States
Orlando, FL
25 June 2022

19135081R00126